SILLY SCARY MONSTER COLORING BOOK FOR KIDS

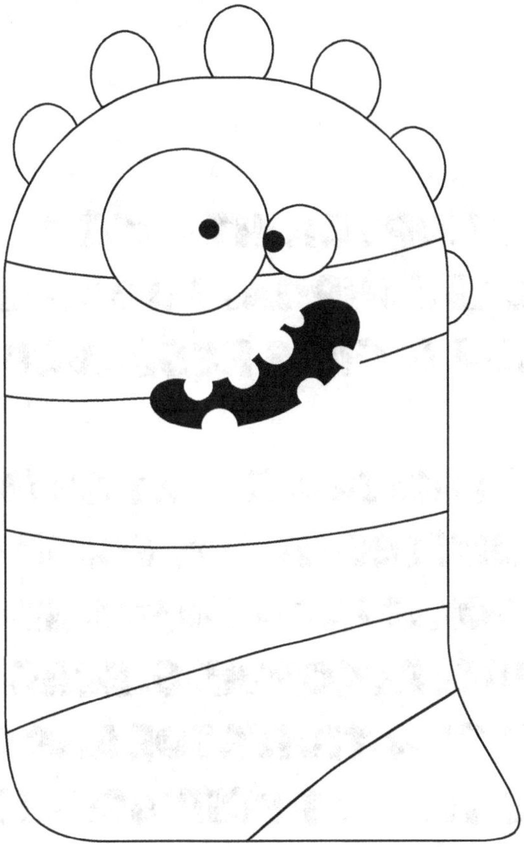

This Monster Coloring Book
Belongs To:

WWW.PRACTICALJOURNALSANDPLANNERS.COM

Cut out this page, following the line, and place the page under your drawing to color it safely.

It is best practice to use crayons, colored pencils, gel /glitter pens for coloring this book instead of using markers or watercolor paints.

Name Your Monster in the Nameplate on the page!

MY NAME IS:

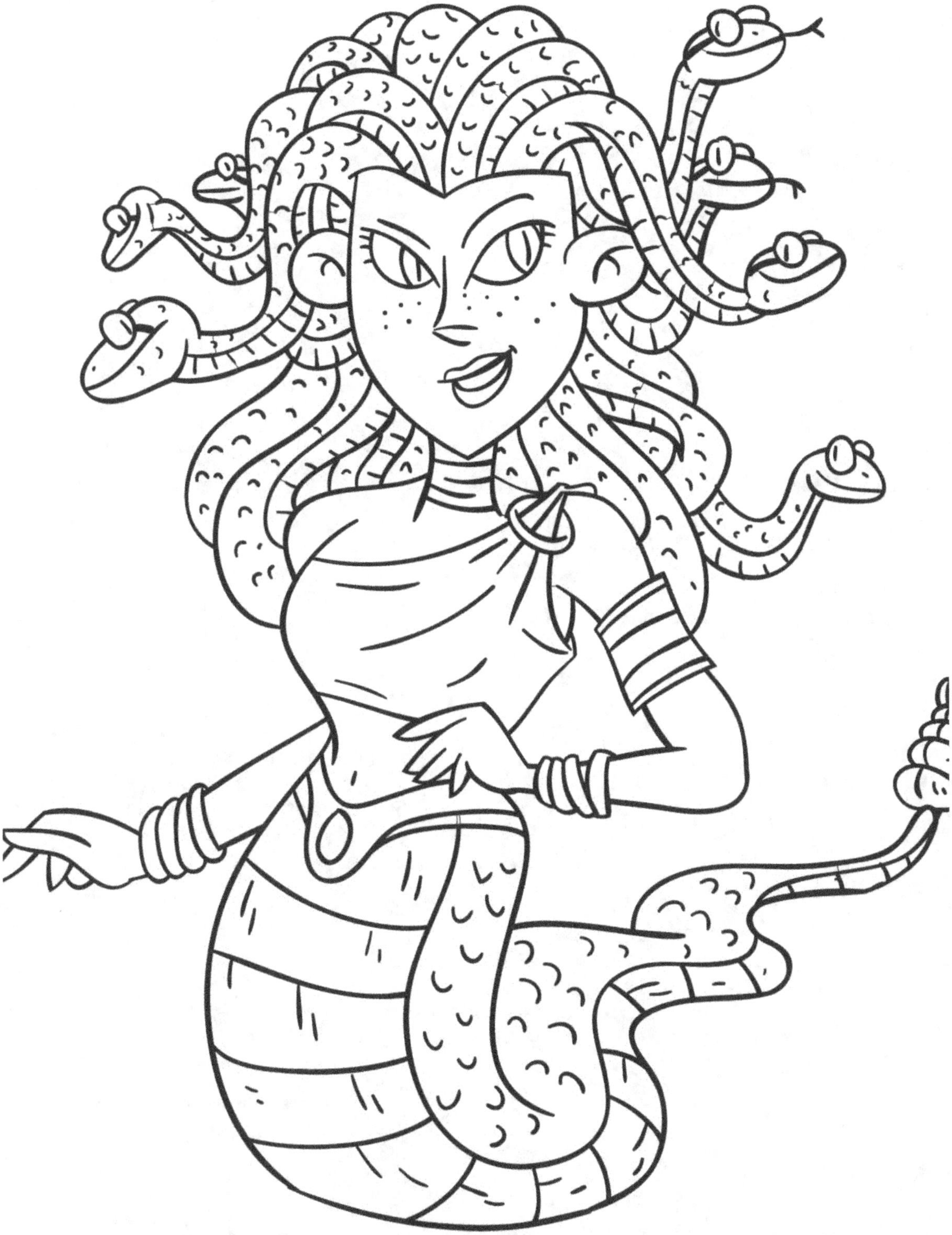

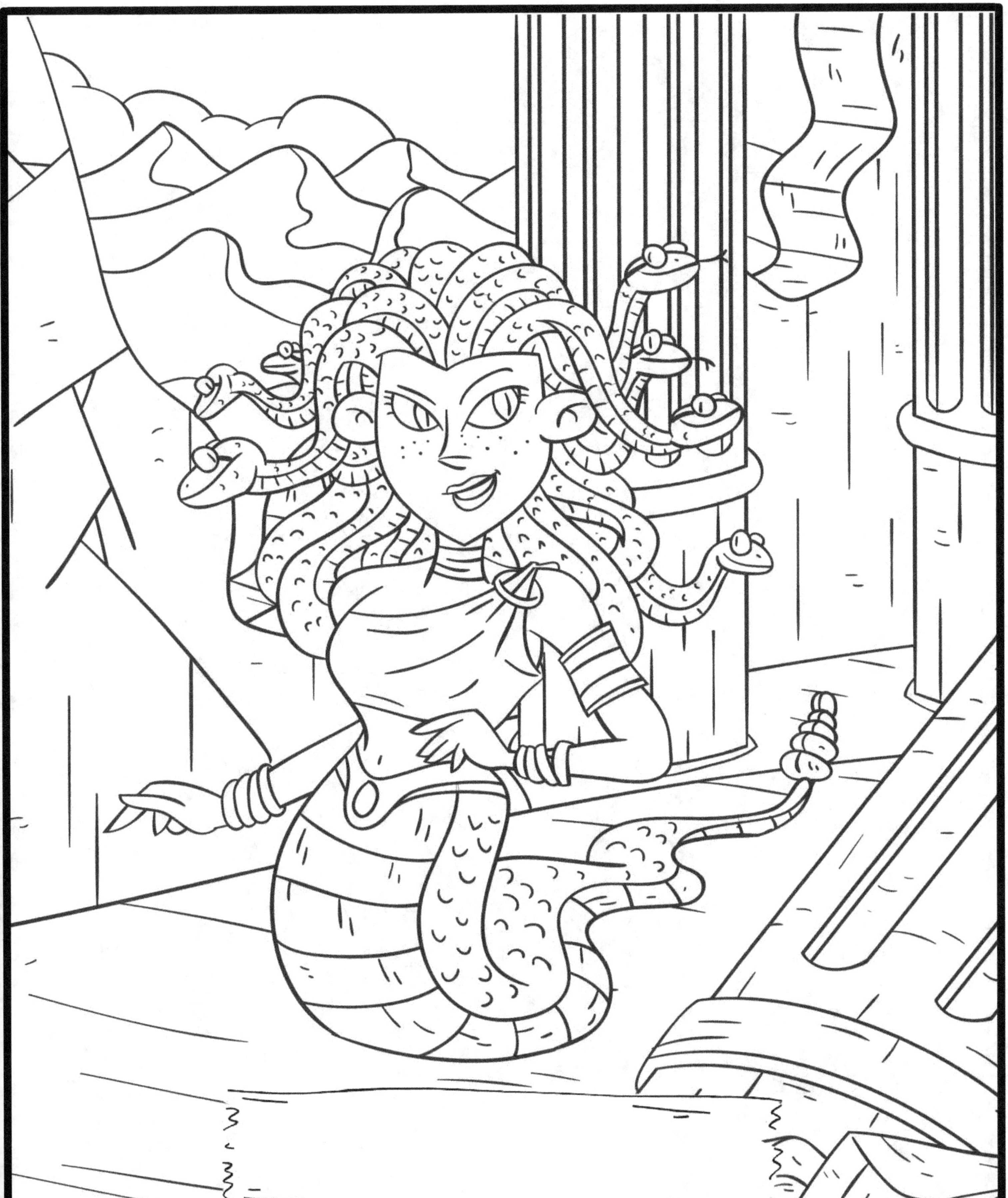

MY NAME IS:

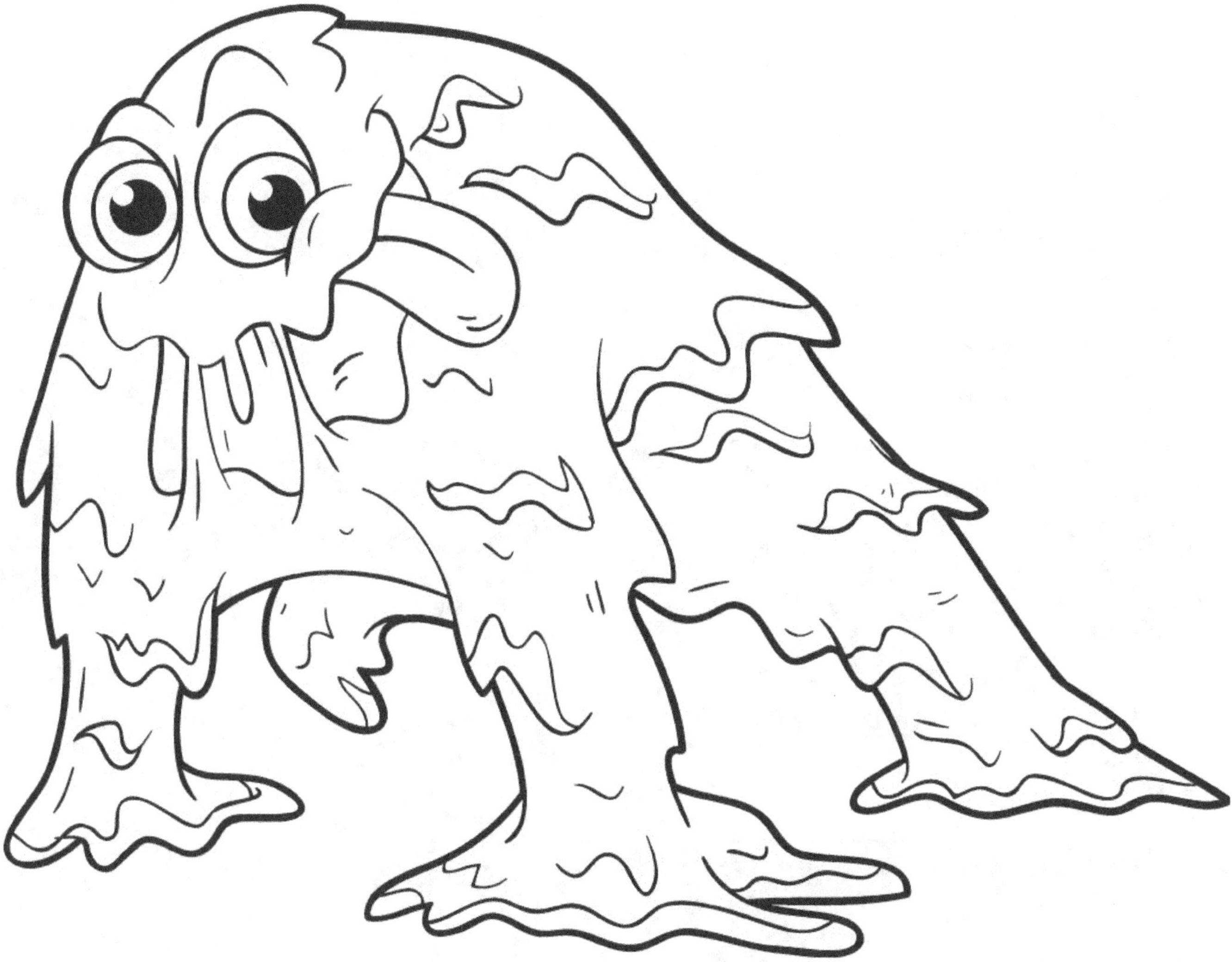

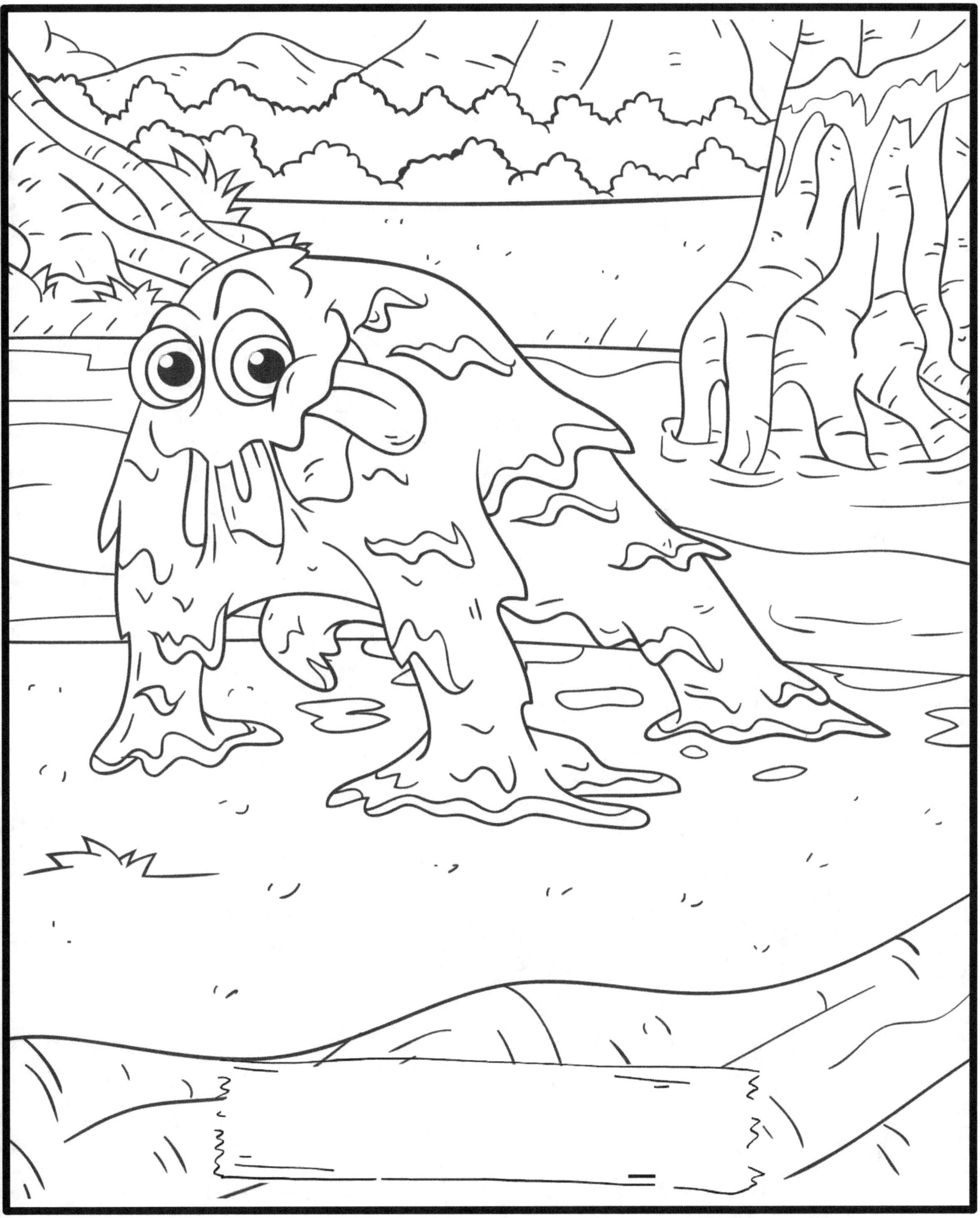

MY NAME IS:

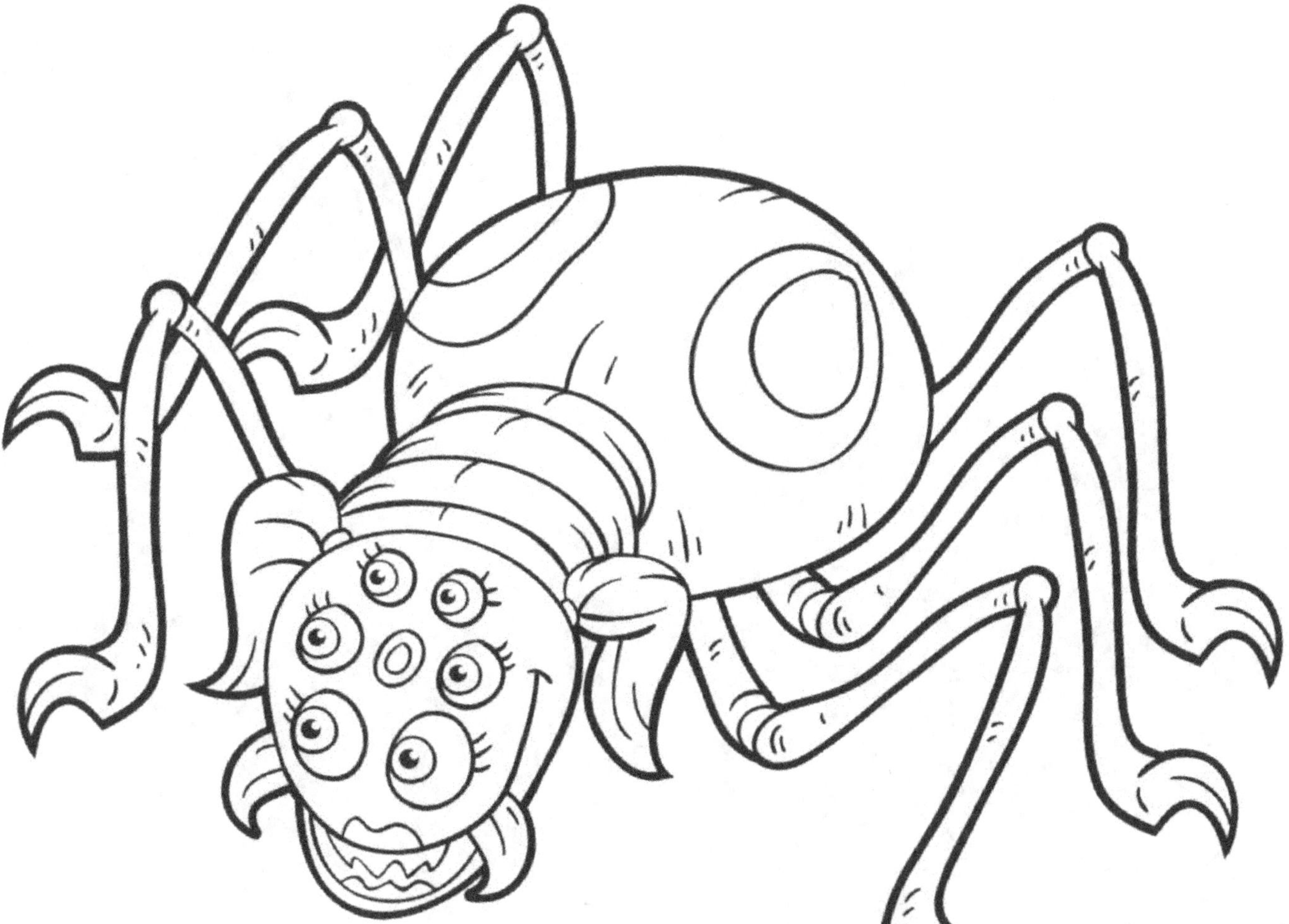

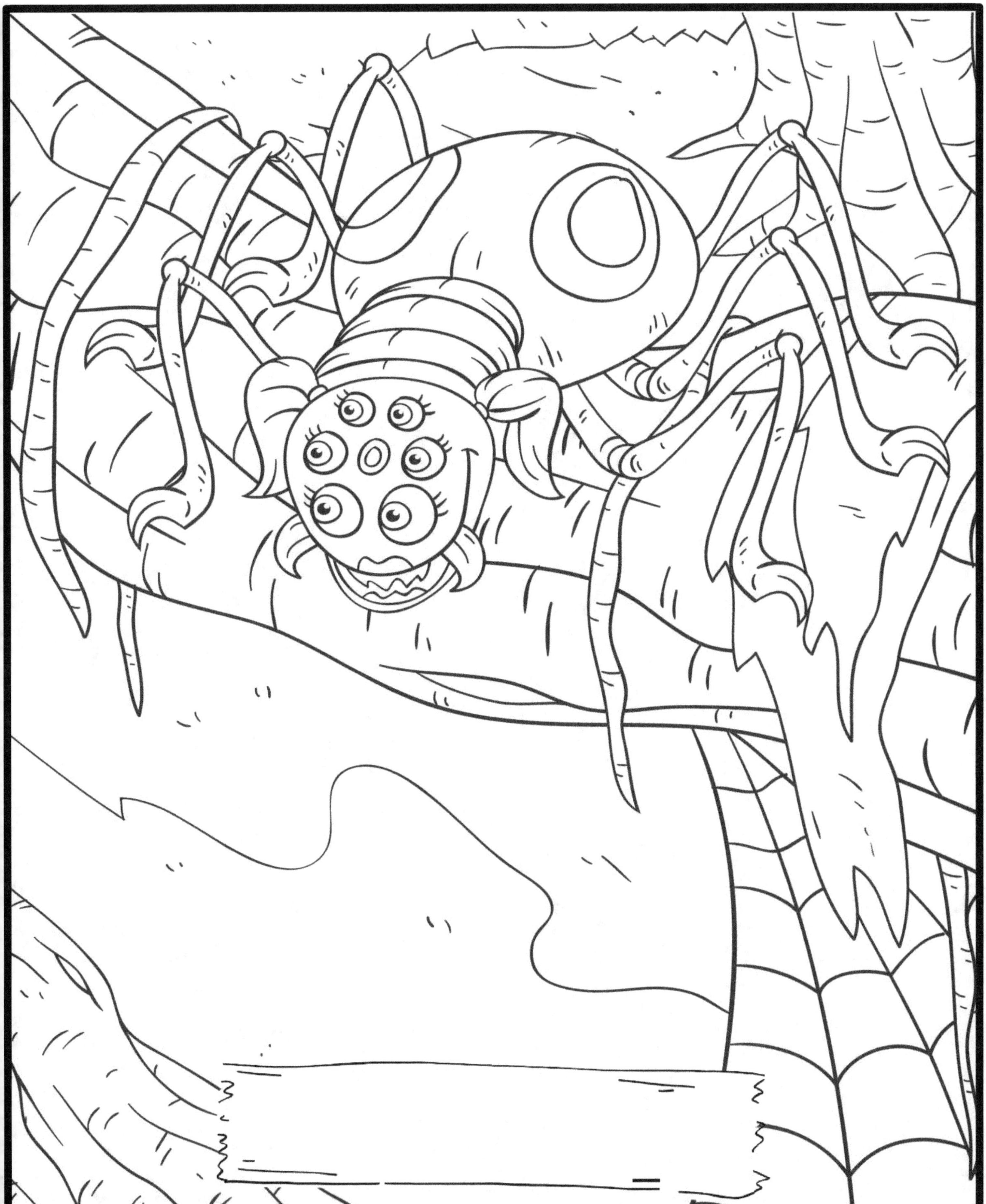

MY NAME IS:

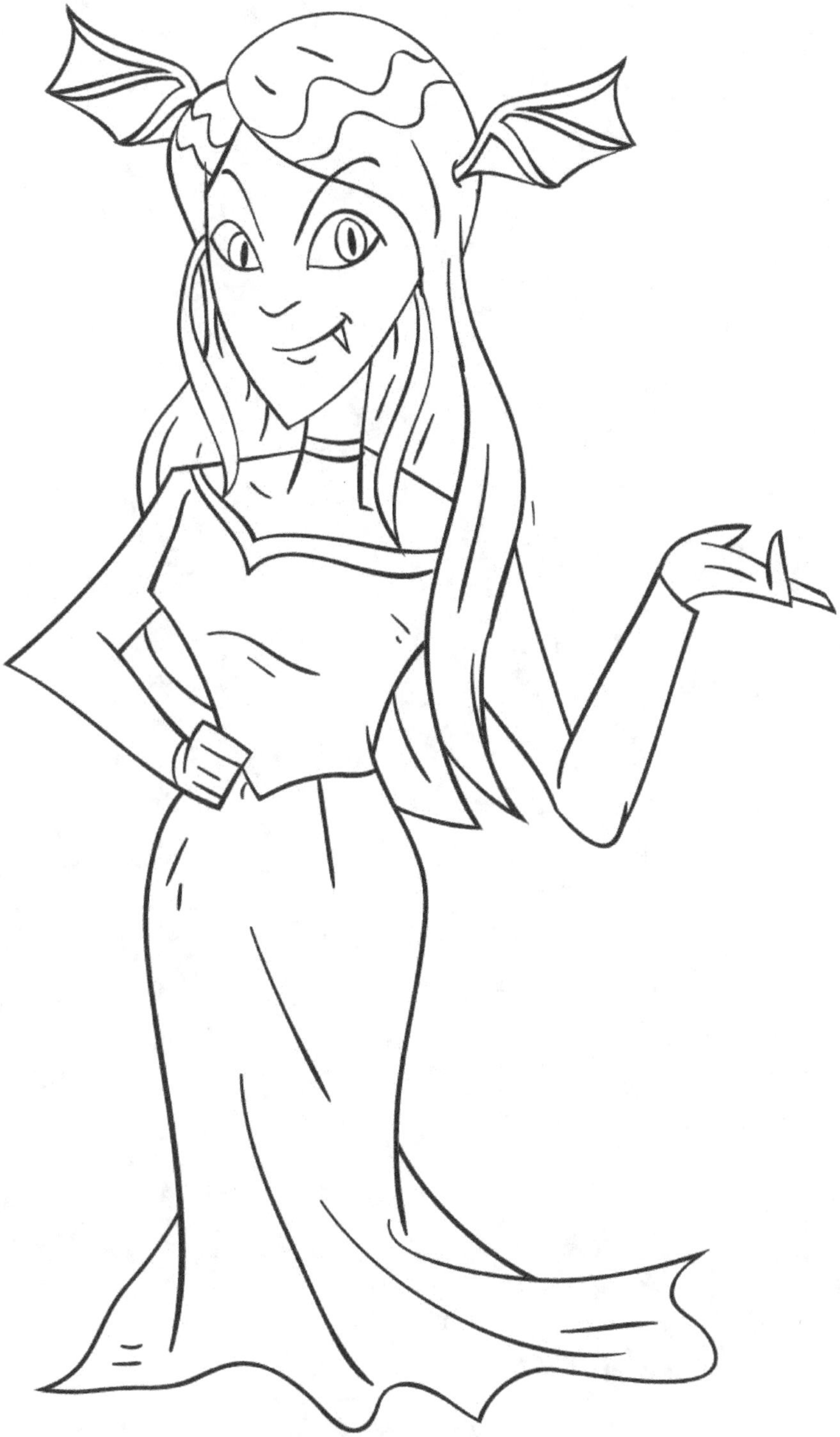

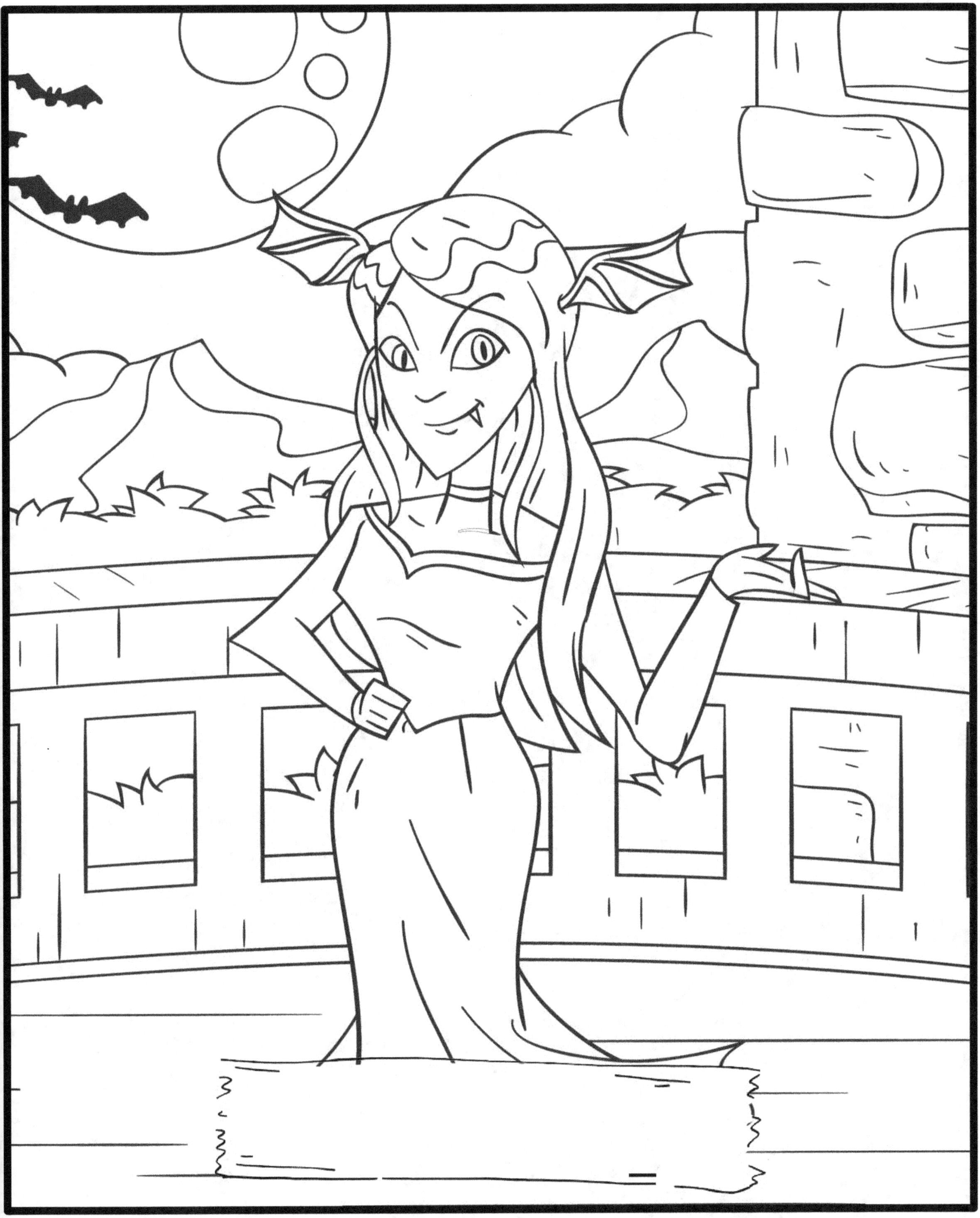

MY NAME IS:

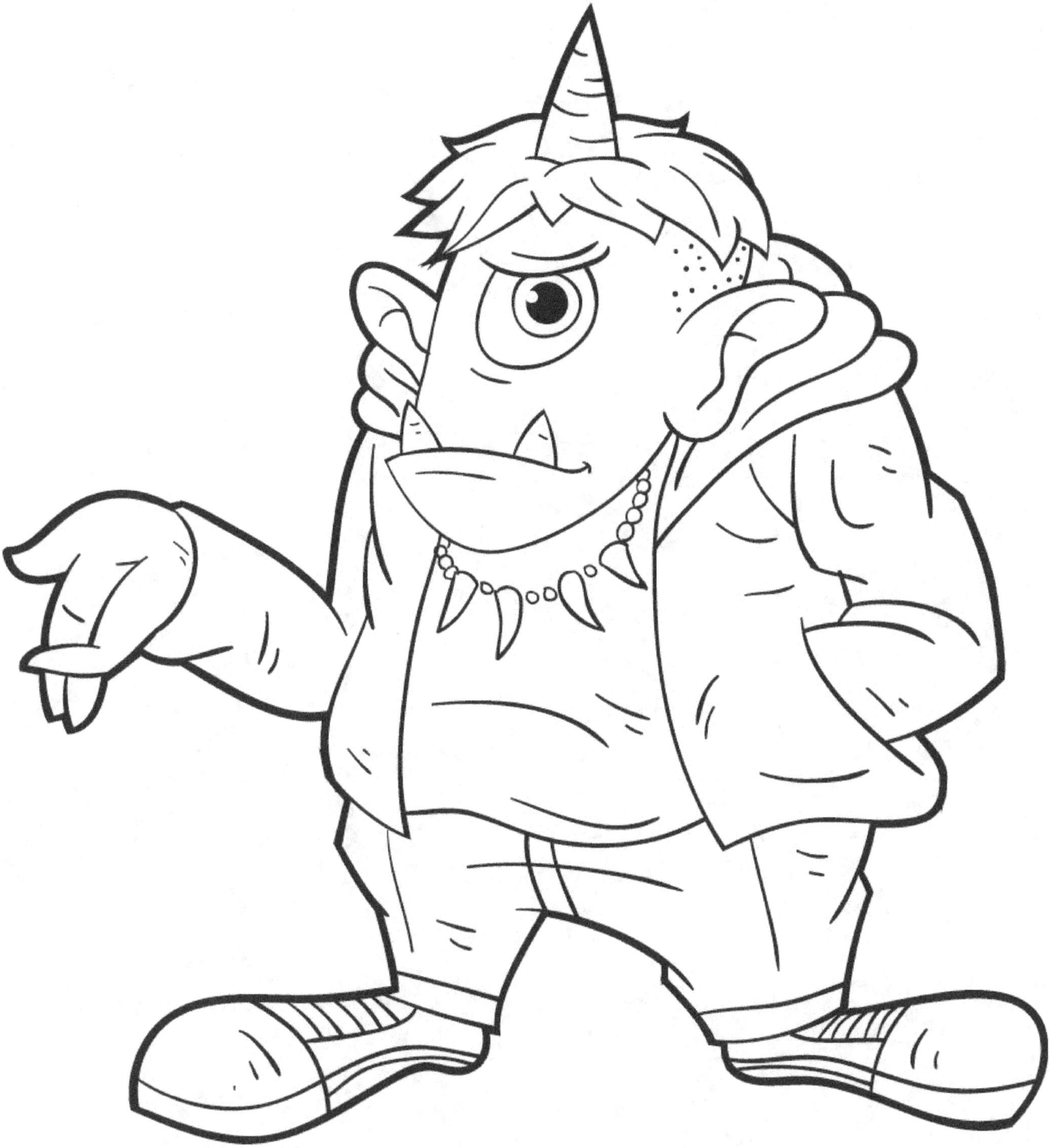

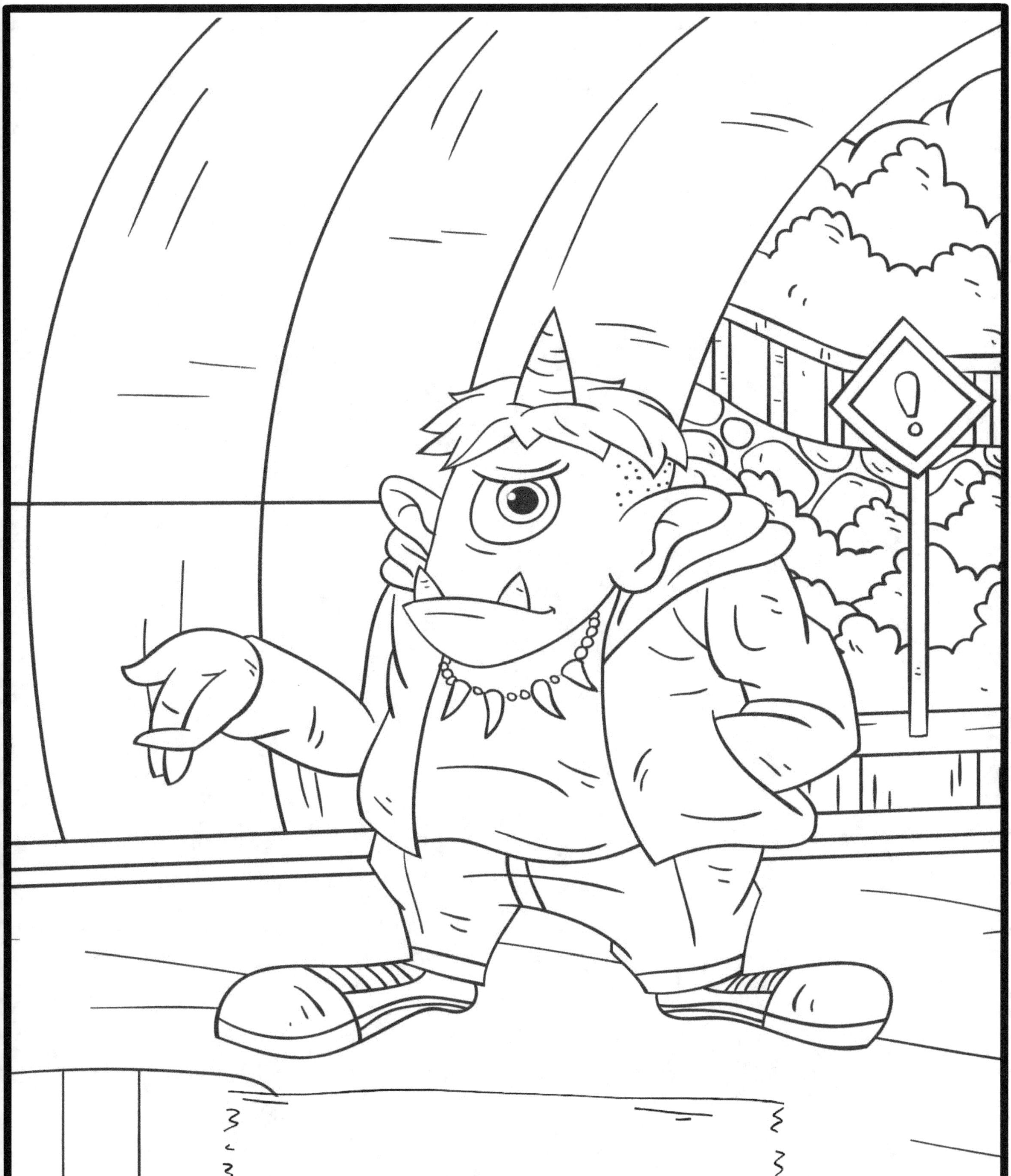

MY NAME IS:

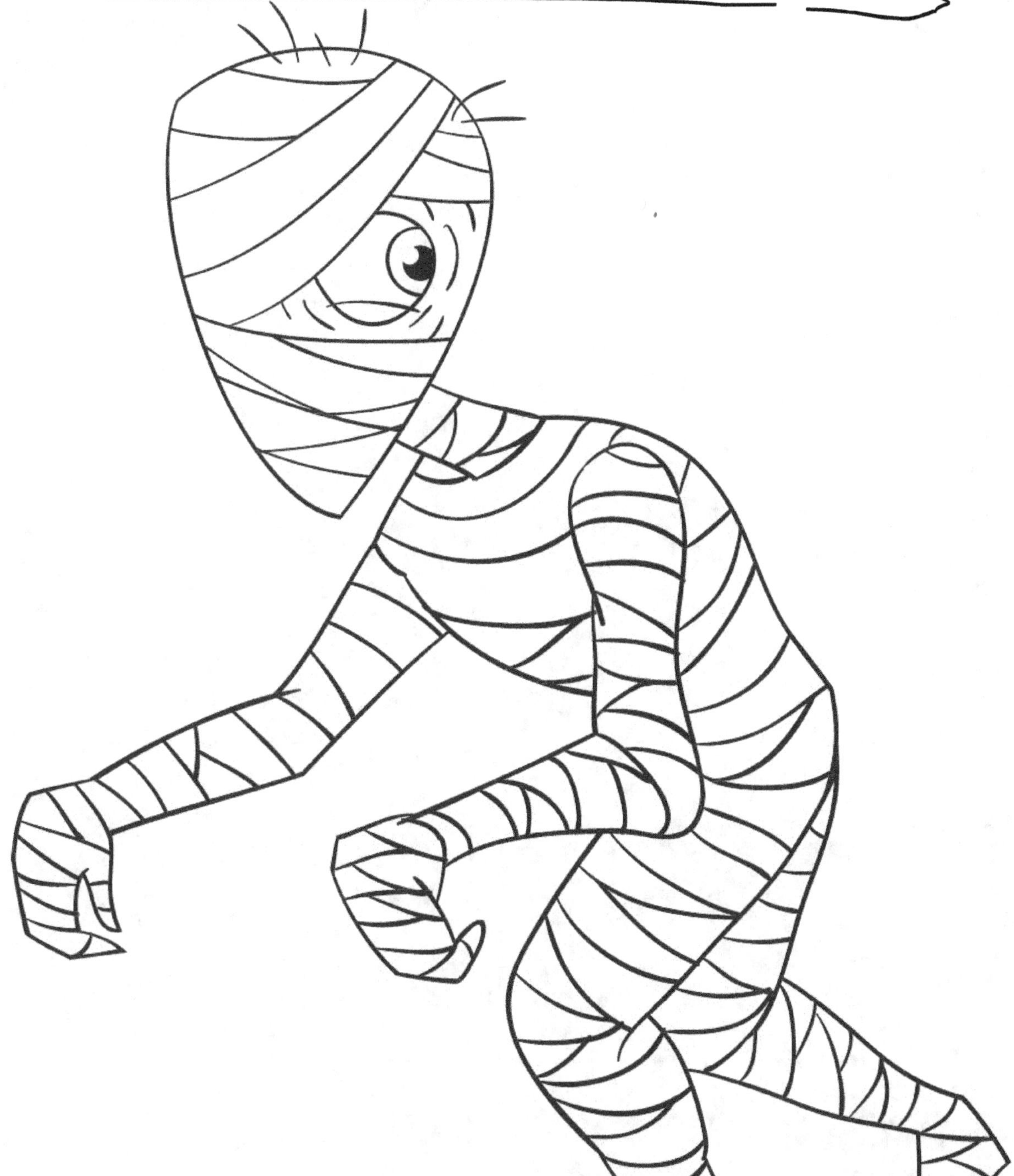

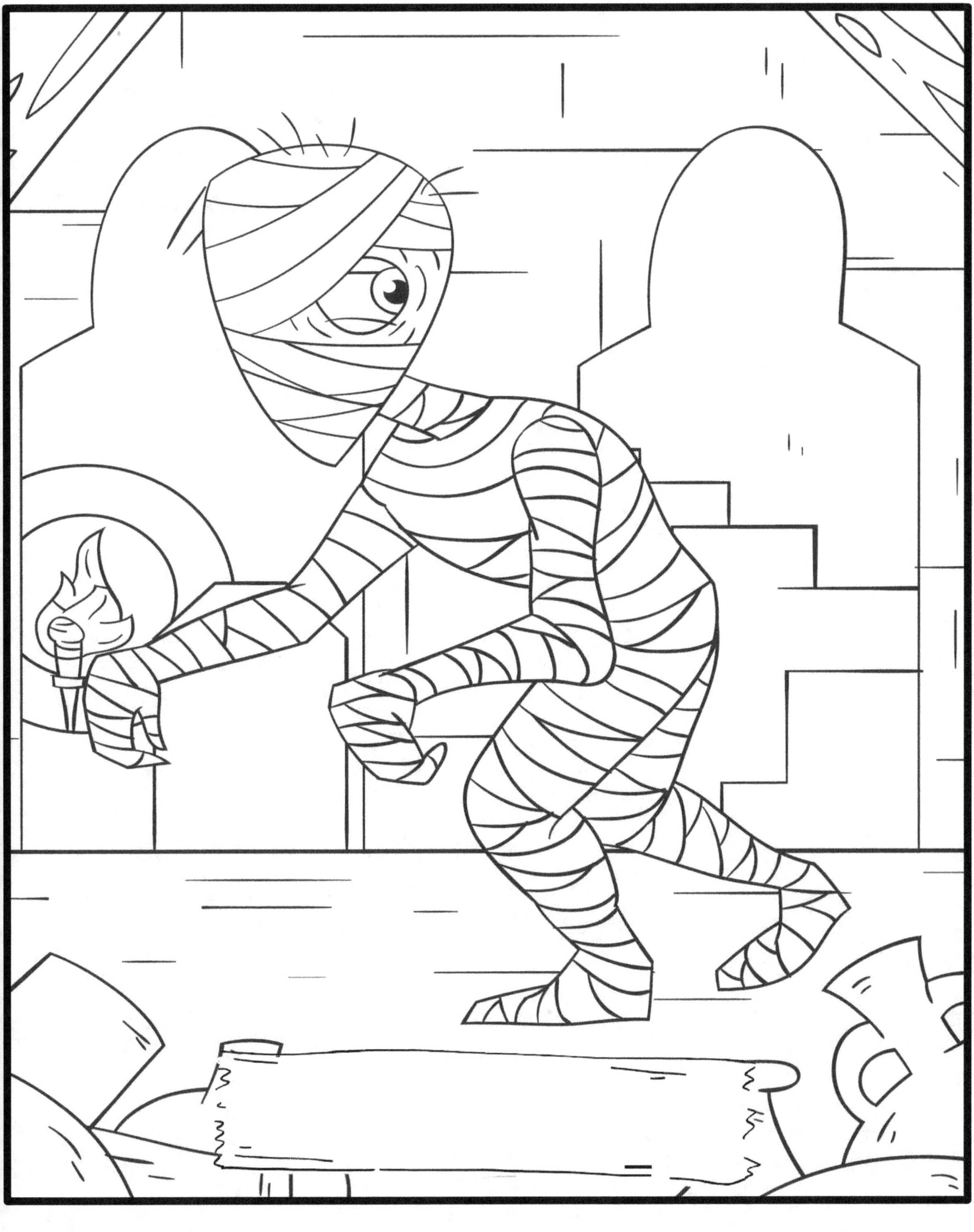

MY NAME IS:

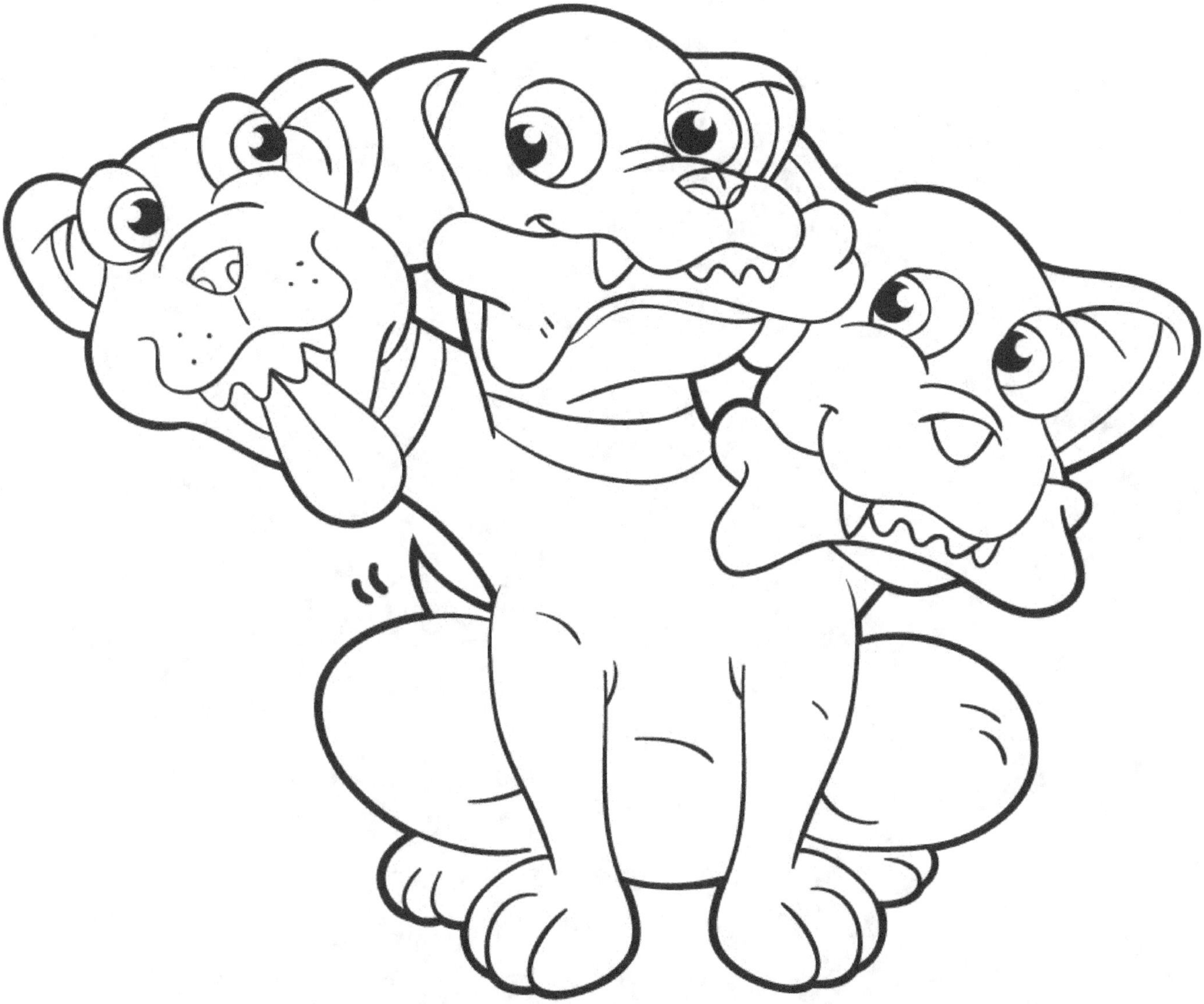

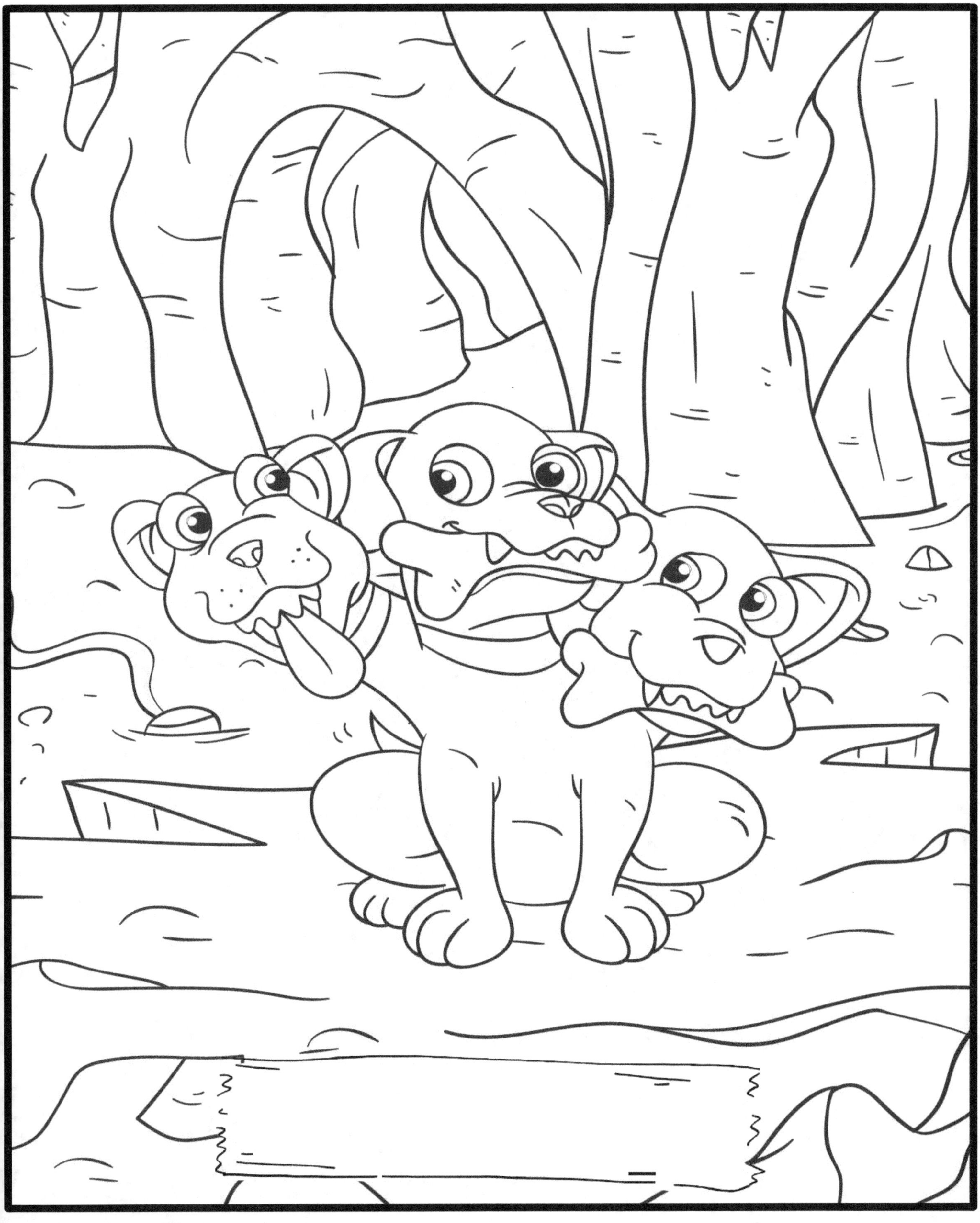

MY NAME IS:

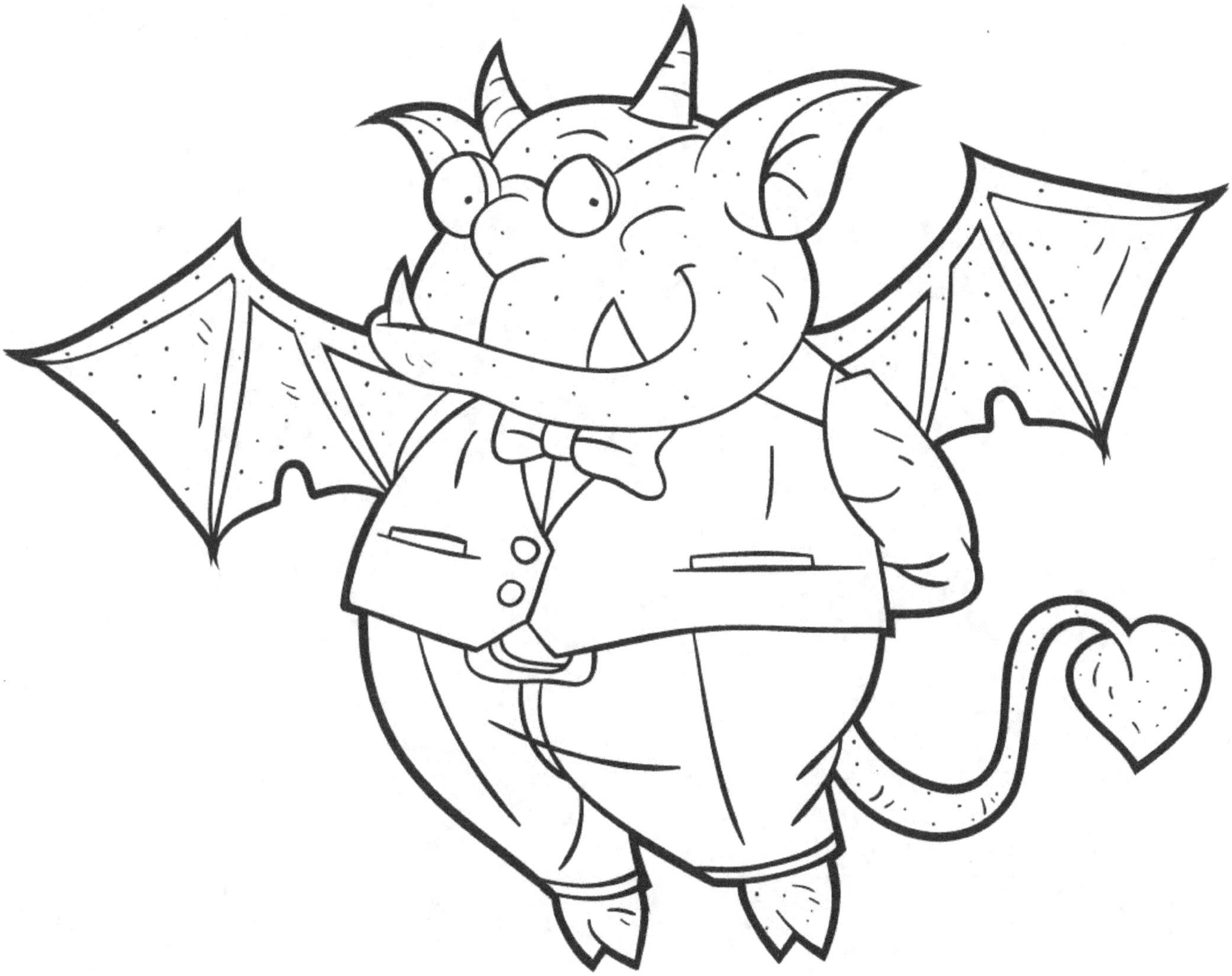

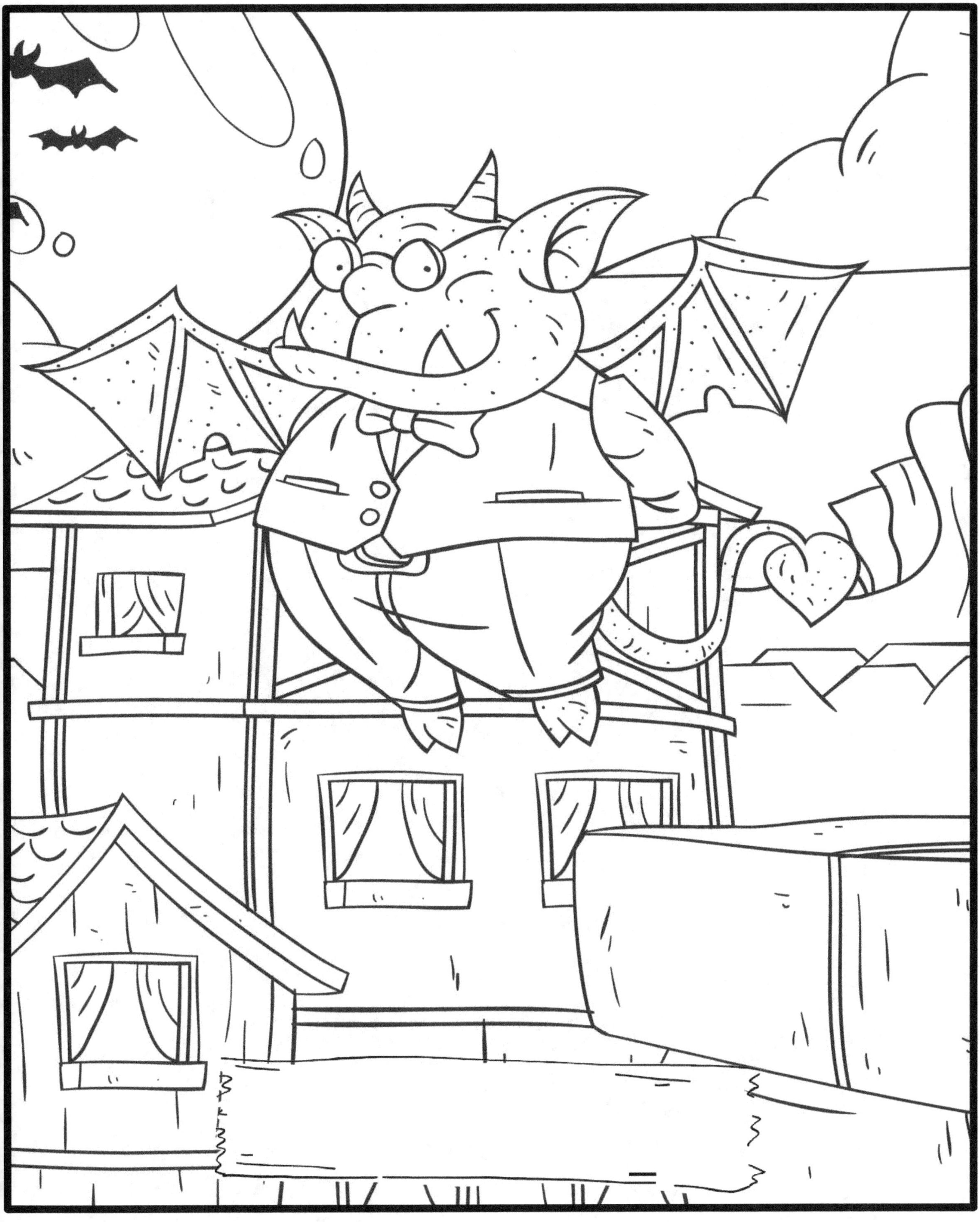

MY NAME IS:

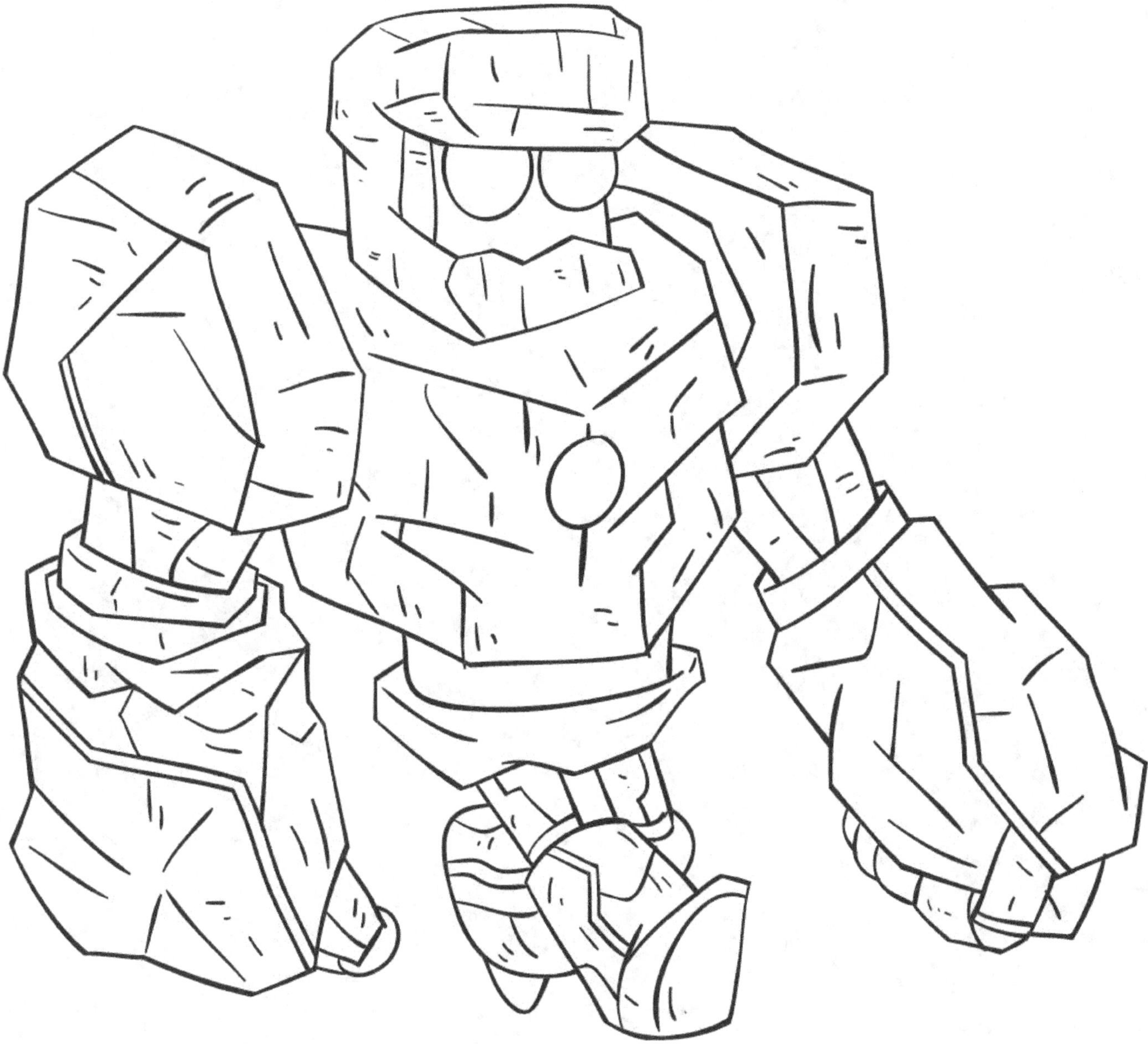

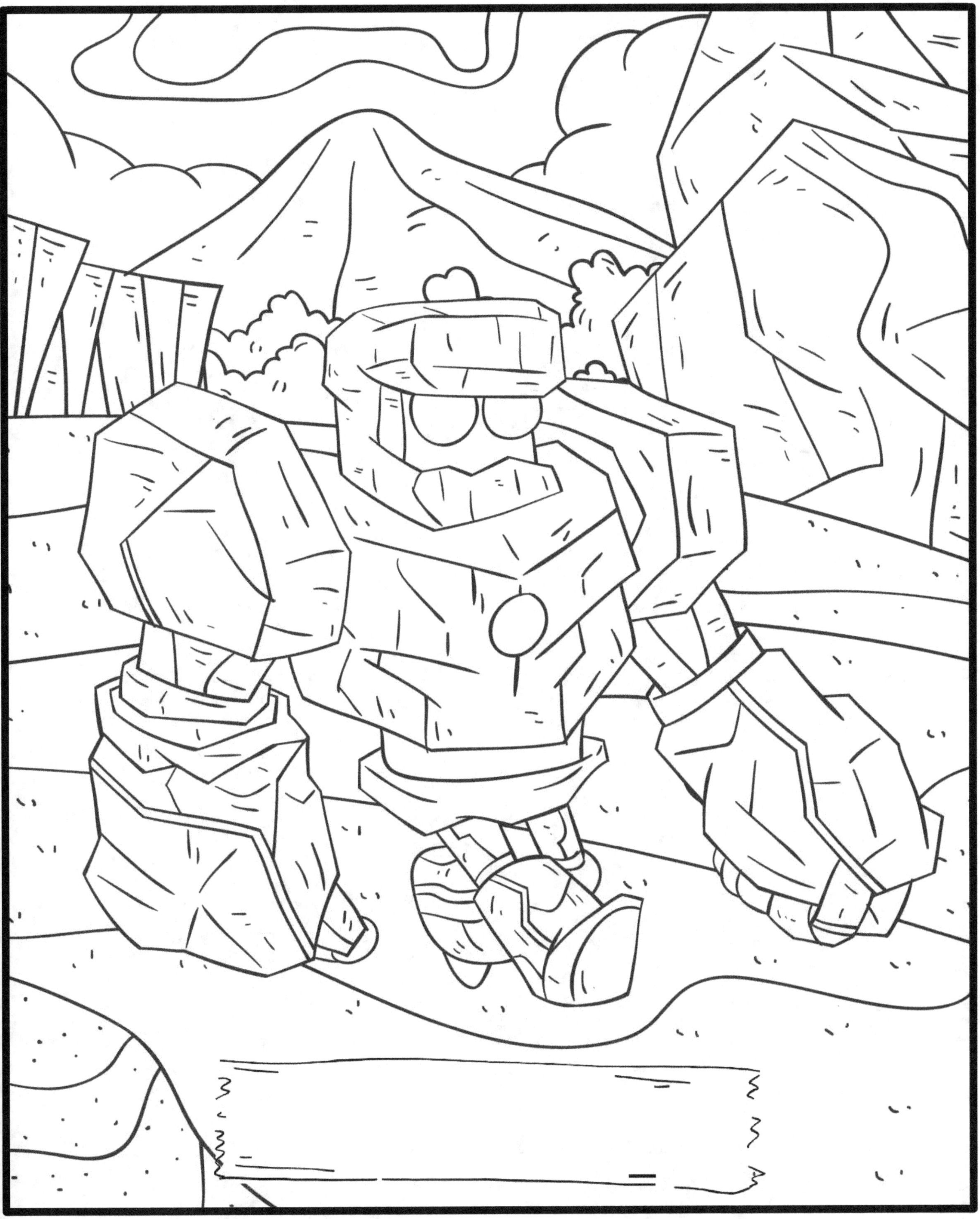

MY NAME IS:

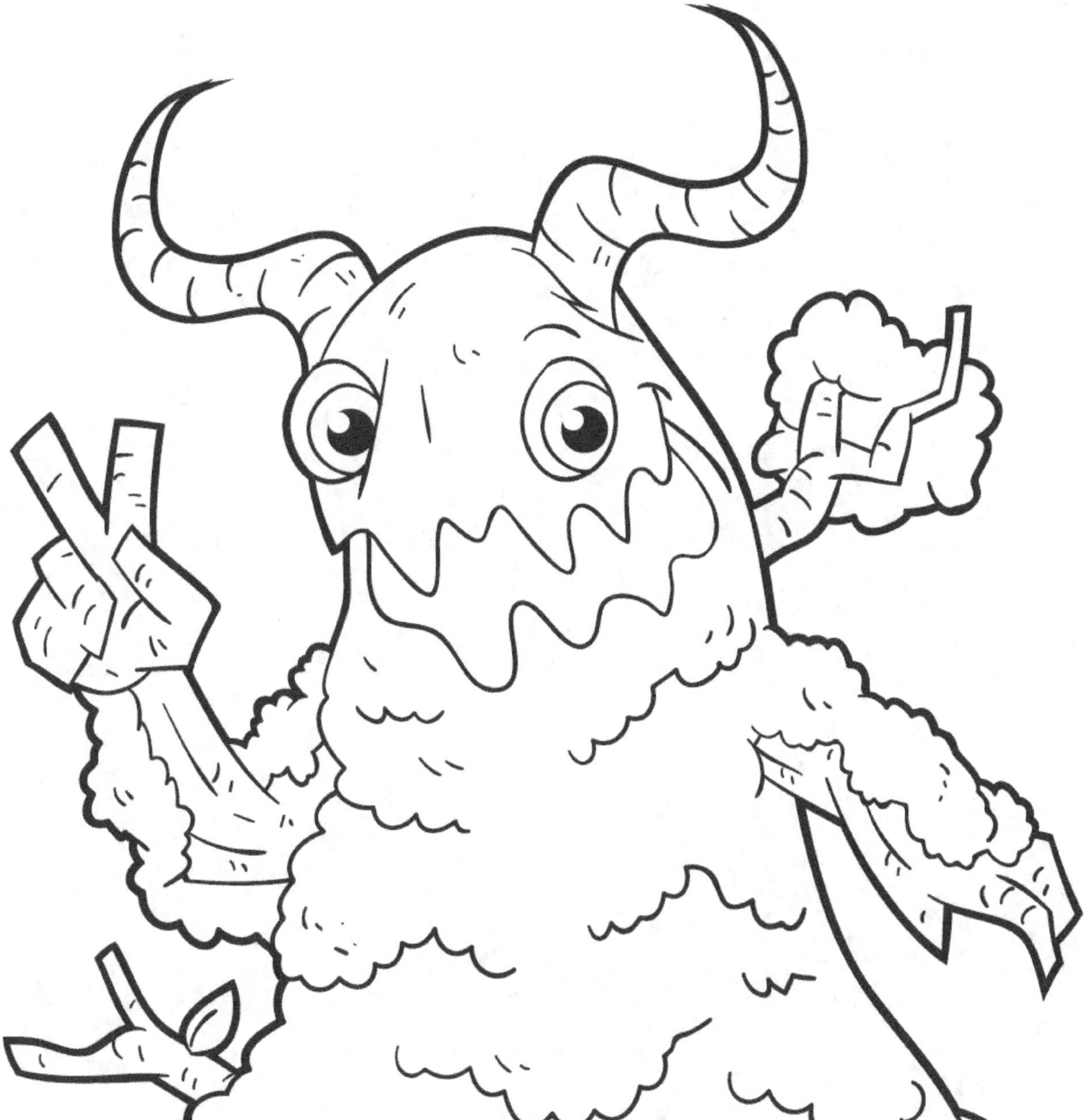

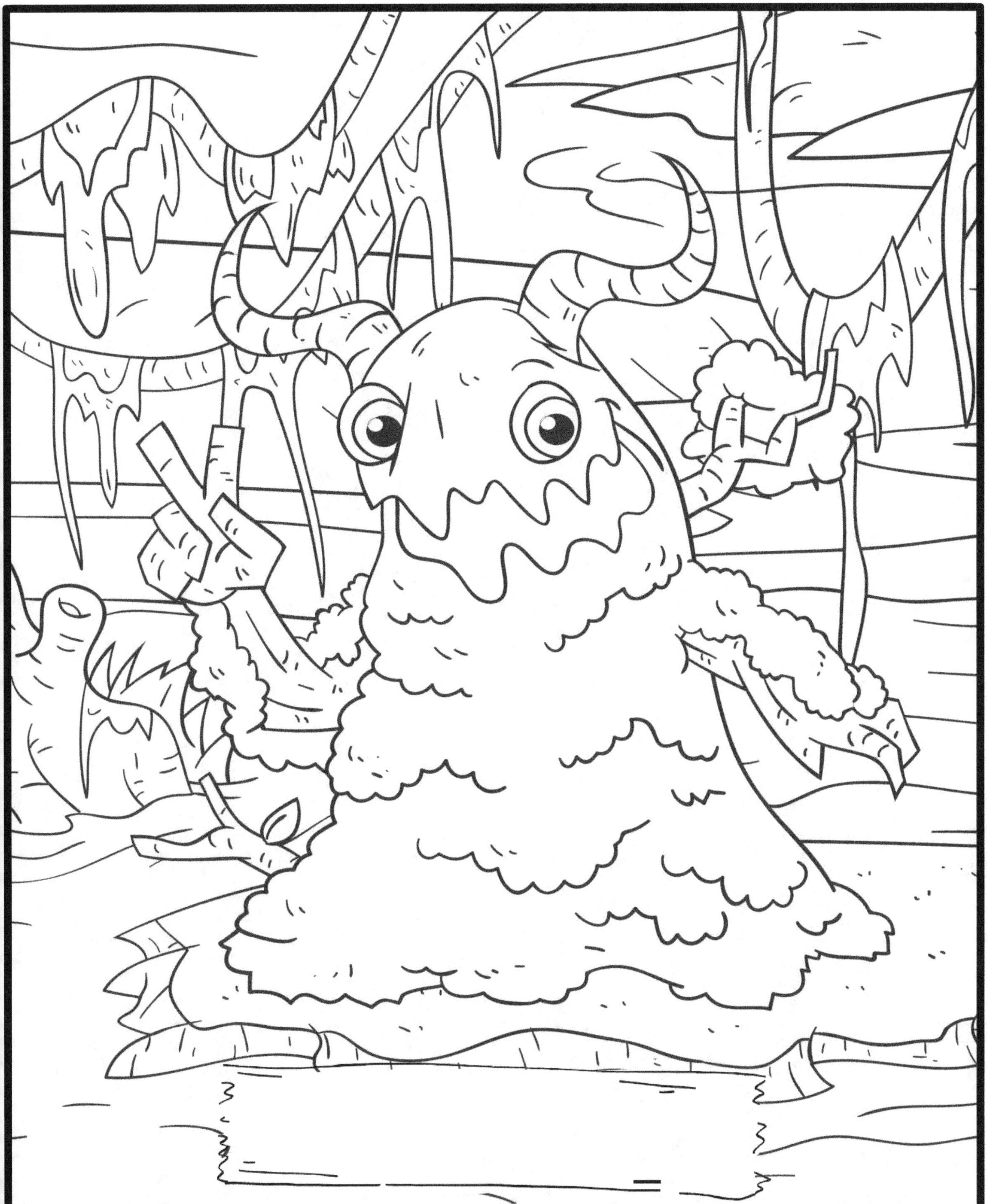

MY NAME IS:

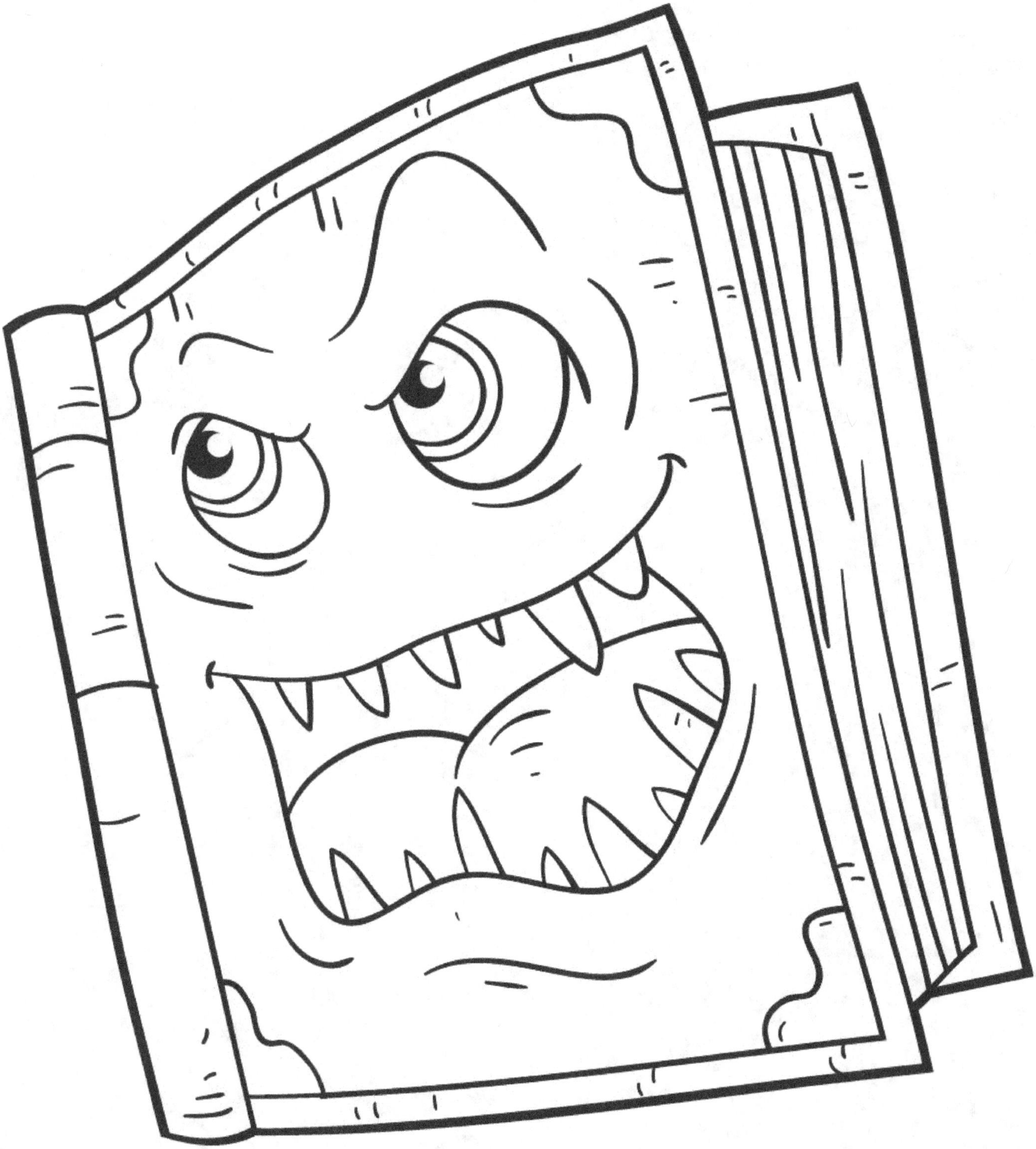

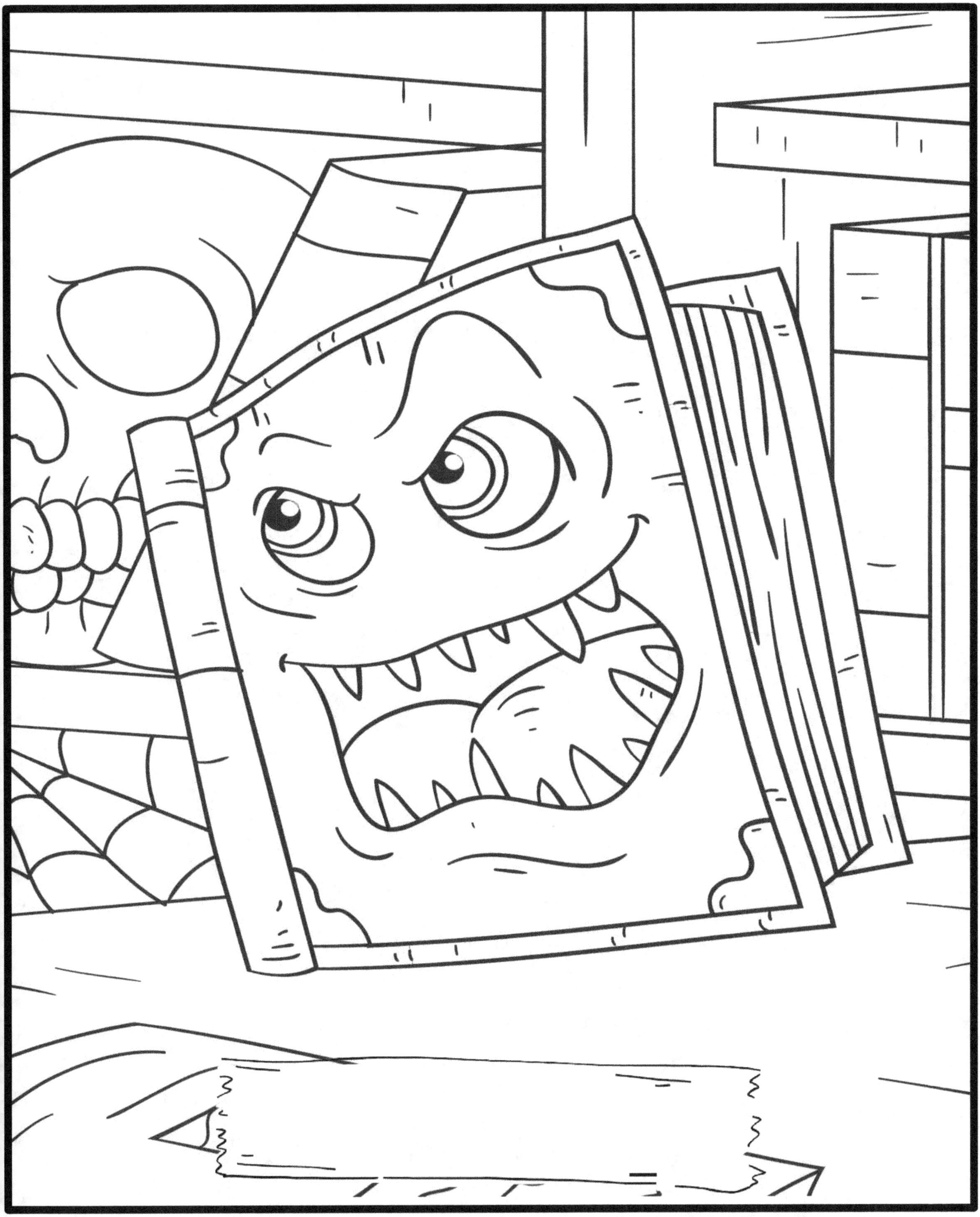

MY NAME IS:

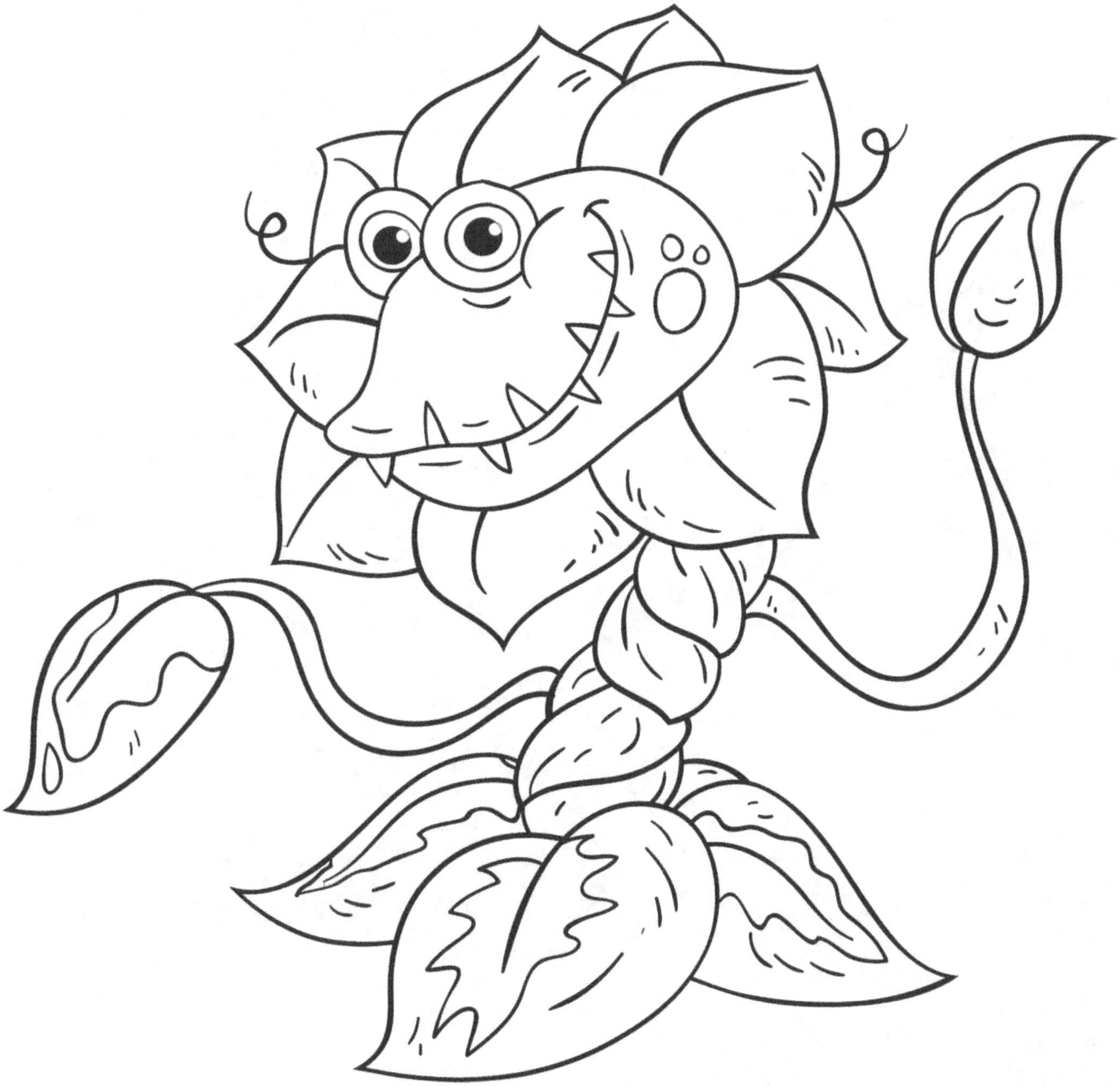

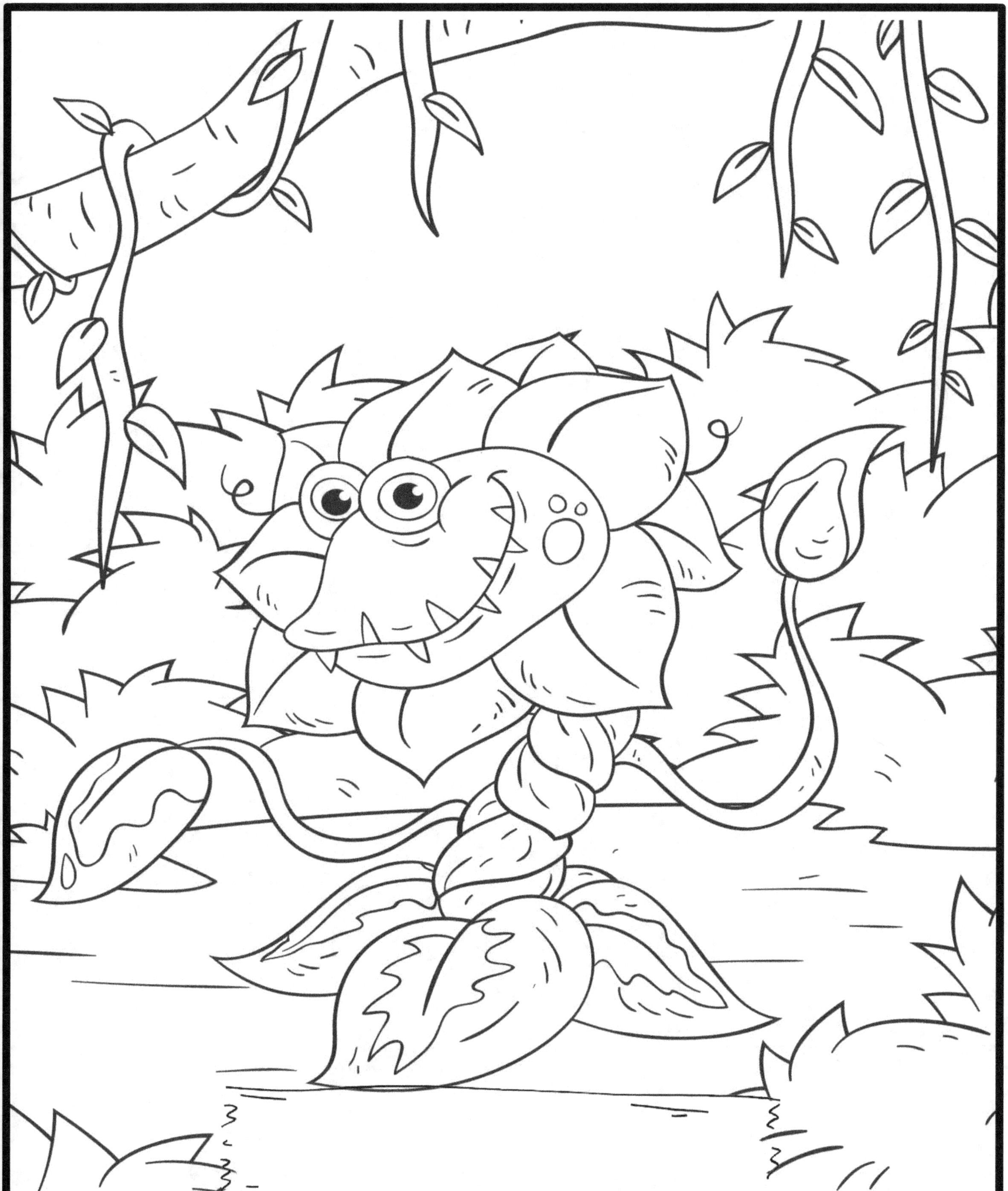

MY NAME IS:

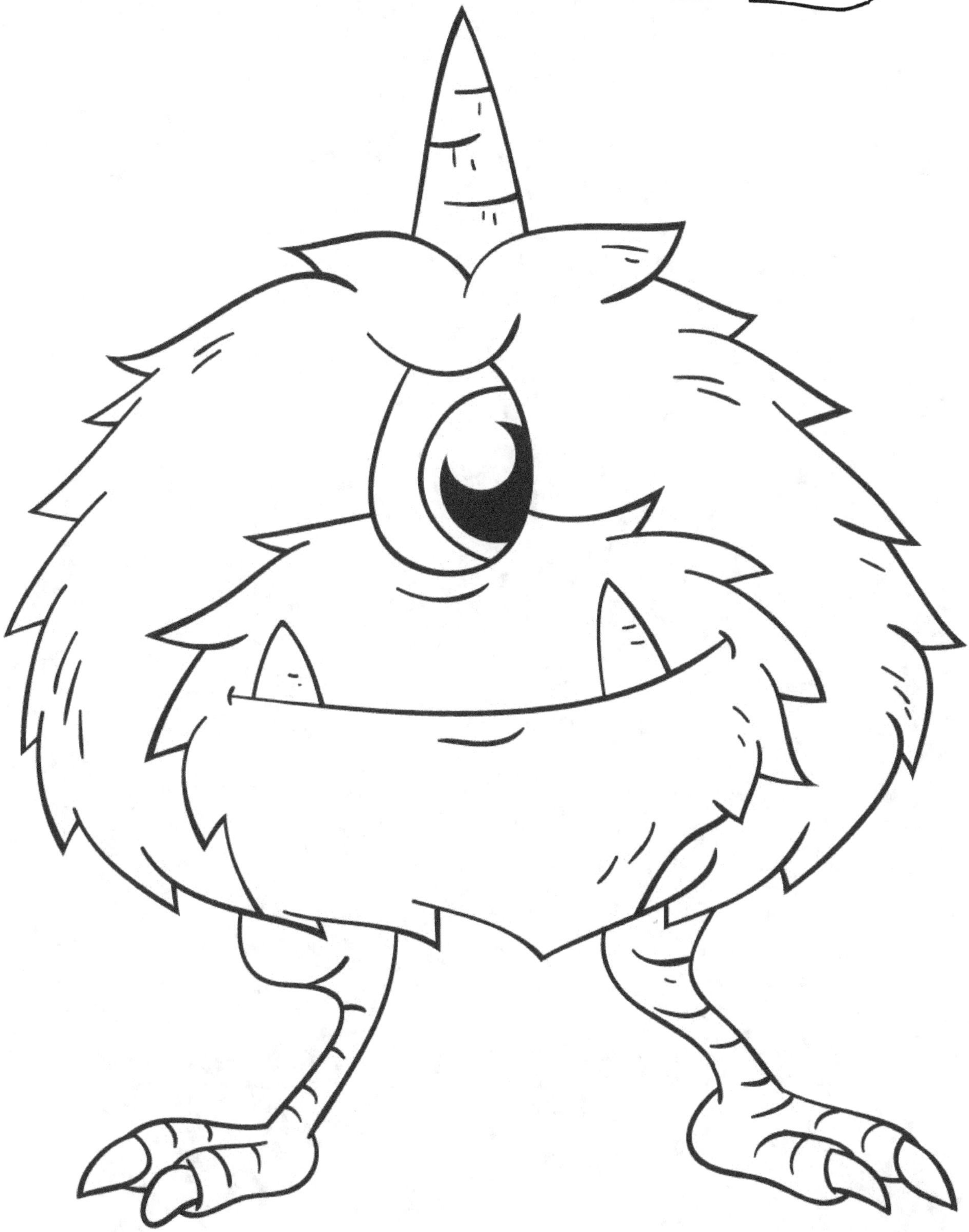

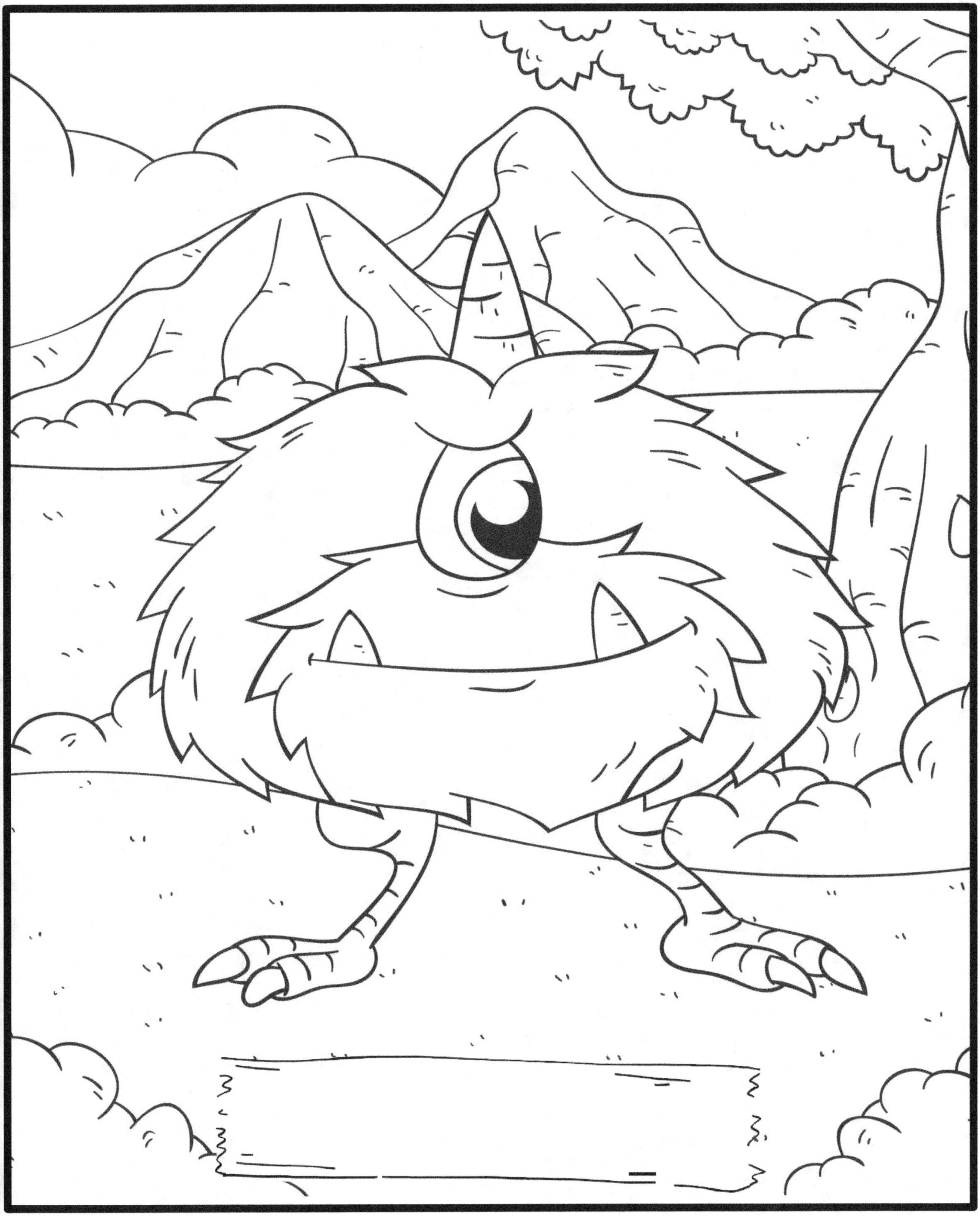

MY NAME IS:

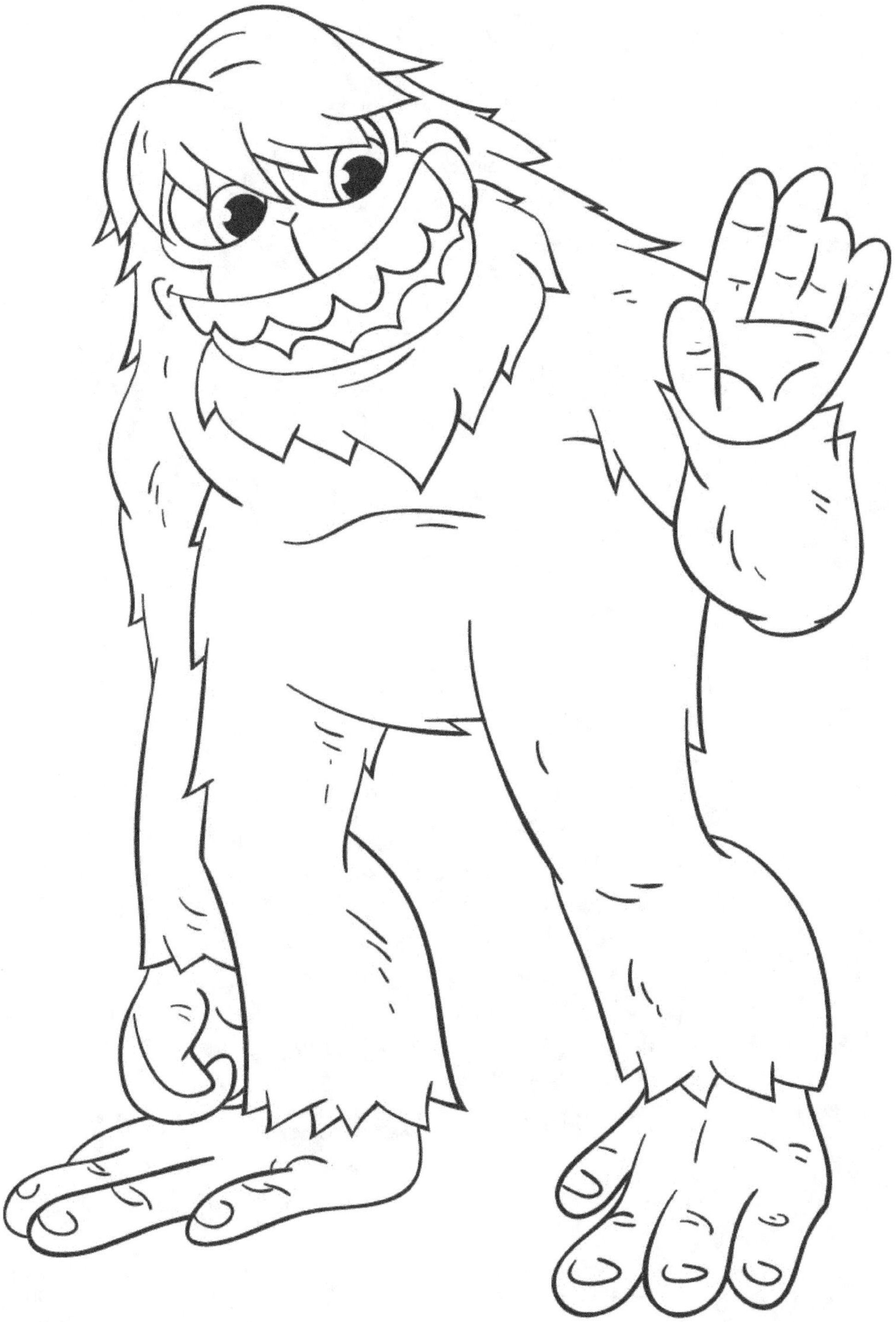

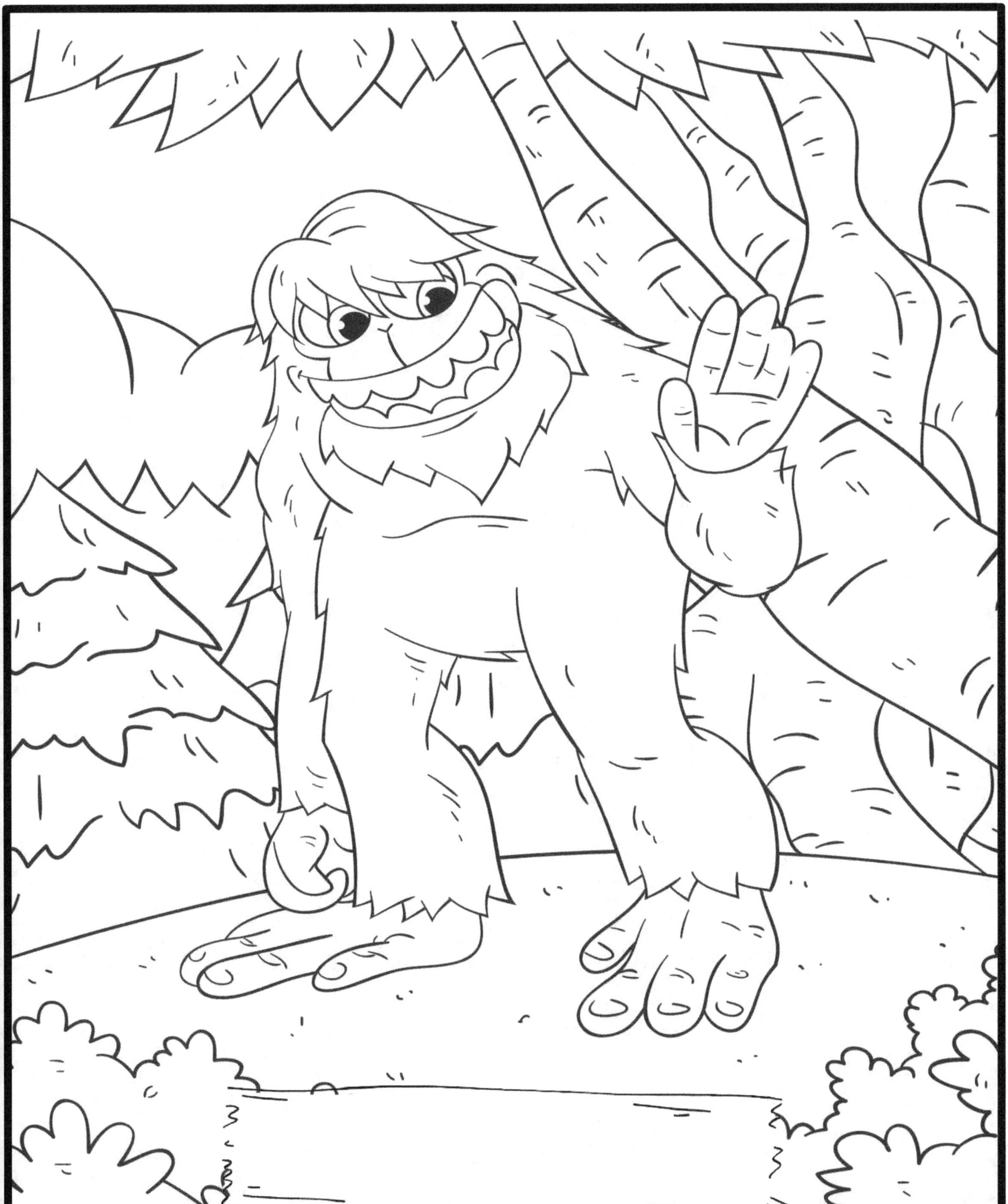

MY NAME IS:

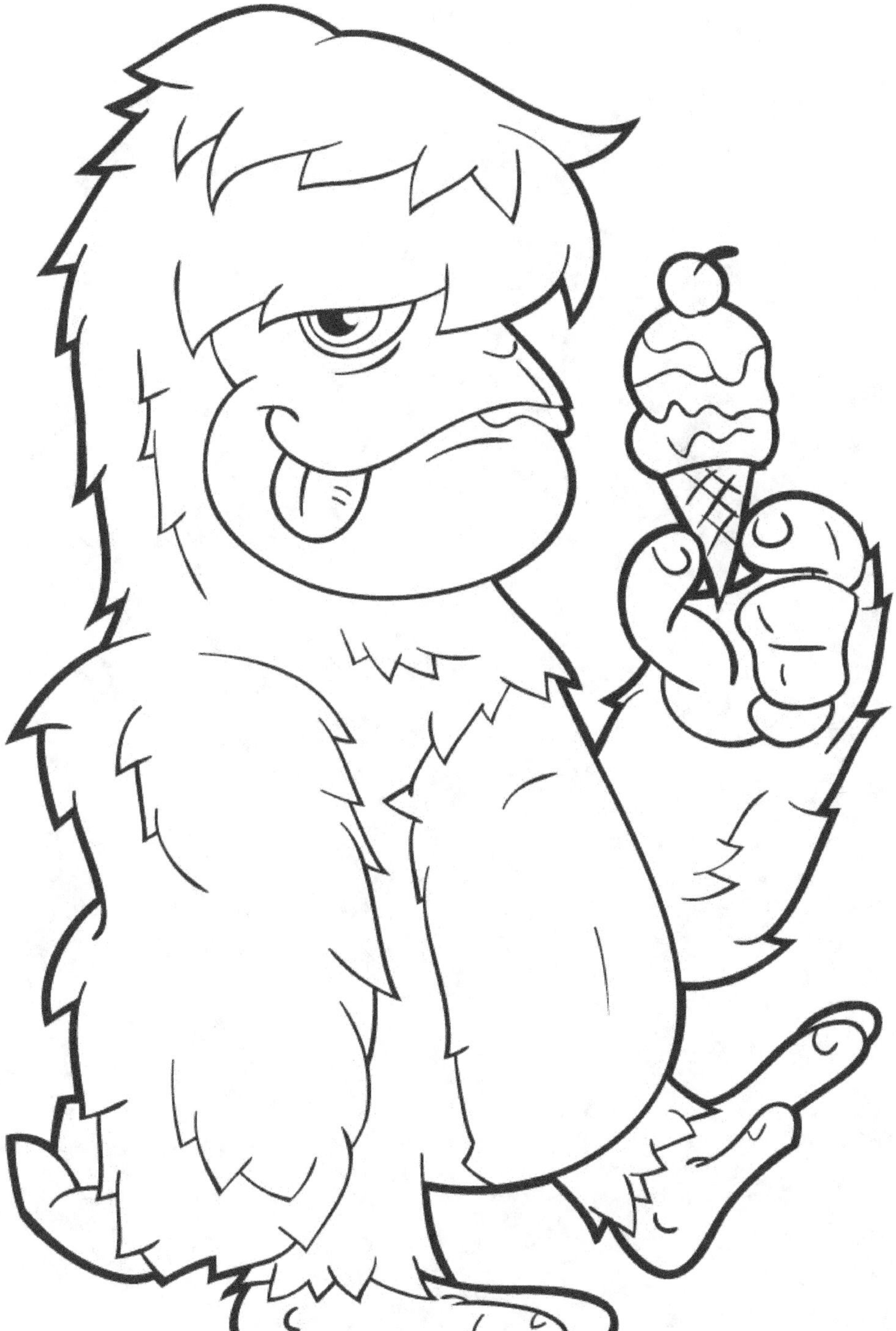

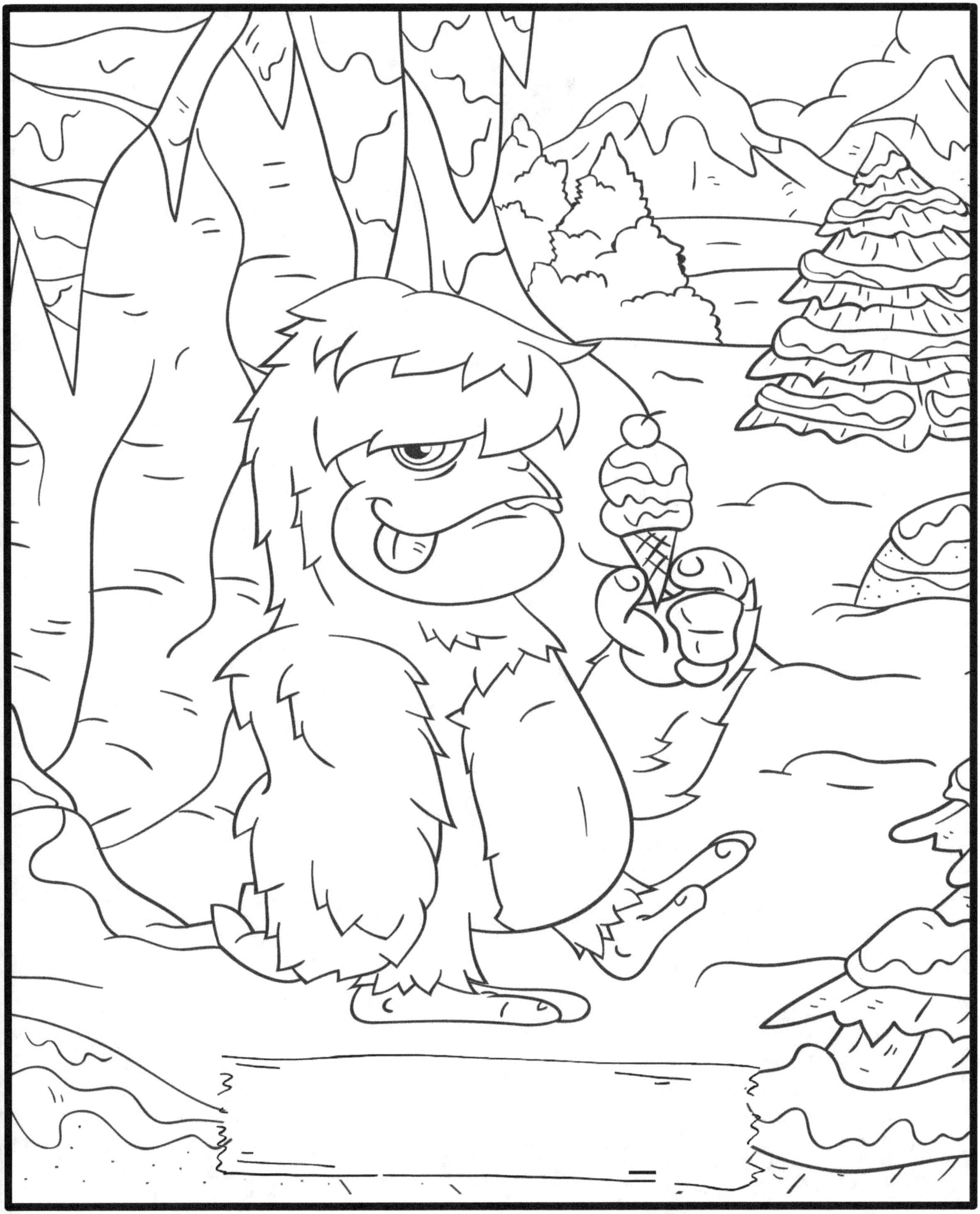

MY NAME IS:

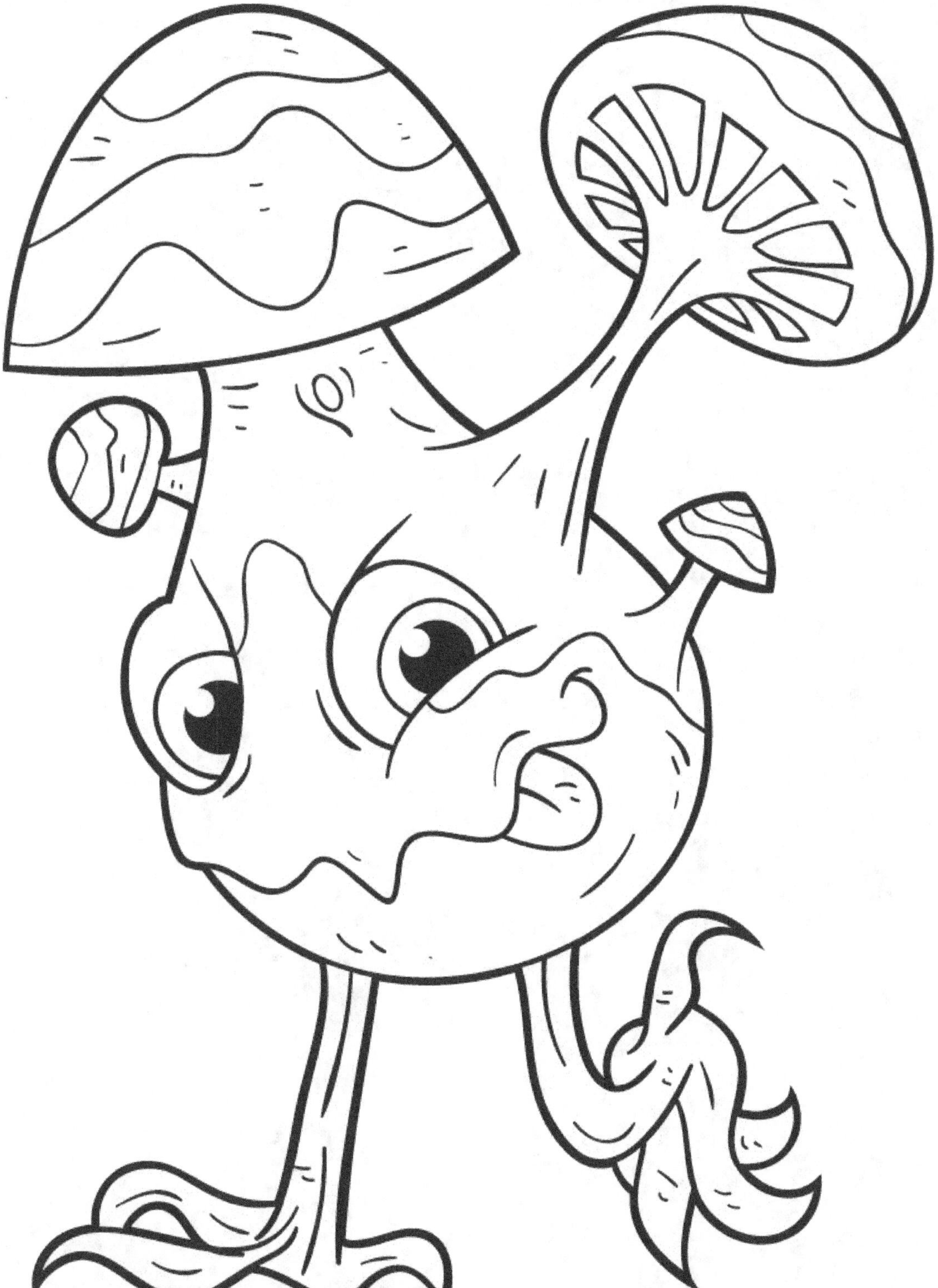

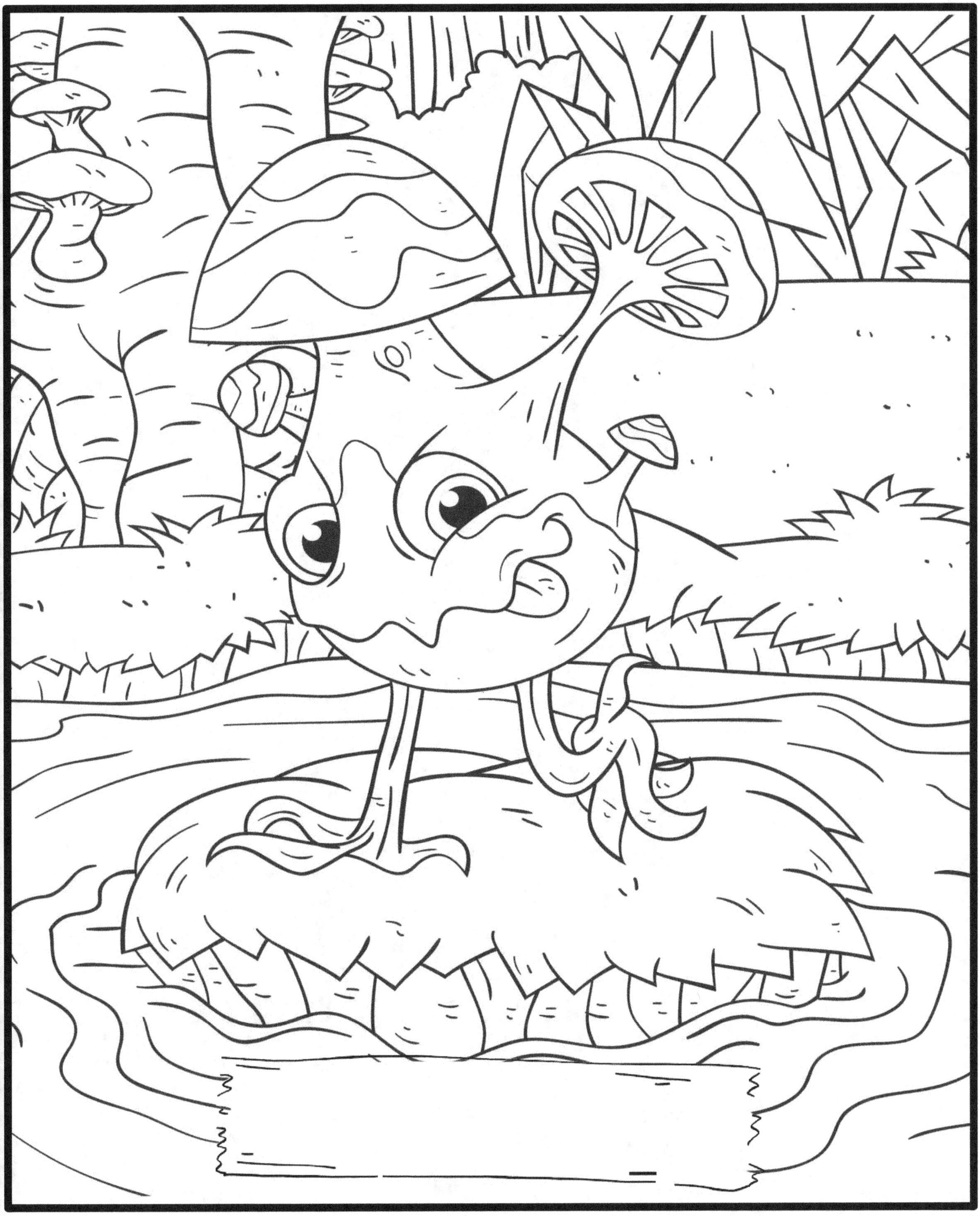

• CIAO •

Thank you for your patronage!

TIME TO BUY ANOTHER BOOK!

Practical Journals and Planners Press

PRACTICALJOURNALSANDPLANNERS.COM

www.ingramcontent.com/pod-product-compliance
Lightning Source LLC
Chambersburg PA
CBHW080525220526
45465CB00006B/2599
9798648260160